D0114008

take
heart

take heart

100 DEVOTIONS
TO SEEING GOD WHEN
LIFE'S NOT OKAY

(in)courage

A DaySpring COMMUNITY

Edited by Grace P. Cho
and Anna E. Rendell

Revell

x

a division of Baker Publishing Group
Grand Rapids, Michigan

© 2020 by DaySpring Cards, Inc.

Published by Revell
a division of Baker Publishing Group
PO Box 6287, Grand Rapids, MI 49516-6287
www.revellbooks.com

Printed in the United States of America

All rights reserved. No part of this publication may be reproduced, stored in a retrieval system, or transmitted in any form or by any means—for example, electronic, photocopy, recording—without the prior written permission of the publisher. The only exception is brief quotations in printed reviews.

Library of Congress Cataloging-in-Publication Data
Names: Cho, Grace P., editor. | Rendell, Anna E., editor.
Title: Take heart : 100 devotions to seeing God when life's not okay / editors,
    Grace P. Cho and Anna E. Rendell.
Description: Grand Rapids, MI : Revell, a division of Baker Publishing Group, 2020. |
    "Edited by Grace P. Cho and Anna E. Rendell."
Identifiers: LCCN 2020006366 | ISBN 9780800738075 (hardcover)
Subjects: LCSH: Devotional literature.
Classification: LCC BV4801 .T35 2020 | DDC 242/.4—dc23
LC record available at https://lccn.loc.gov/2020006366

Unless otherwise indicated, Scripture quotations are from the Holy Bible, New International Version®. NIV®. Copyright © 1973, 1978, 1984, 2011 by Biblica, Inc.™ Used by permission of Zondervan. All rights reserved worldwide. www.zondervan.com. The "NIV" and "New International Version" are trademarks registered in the United States Patent and Trademark Office by Biblica, Inc.™

Scripture quotations labeled CSB are from the Christian Standard Bible®, copyright © 2017 by Holman Bible Publishers. Used by permission. Christian Standard Bible® and CSB® are federally registered trademarks of Holman Bible Publishers.

Scripture quotations labeled ESV are from The Holy Bible, English Standard Version® (ESV®), copyright © 2001 by Crossway, a publishing ministry of Good News Publishers. Used by permission. All rights reserved. ESV Text Edition: 2016

Scripture quotations labeled KJV are from the King James Version of the Bible.

Scripture quotations labeled MSG are from THE MESSAGE, copyright © 1993, 1994, 1995, 1996, 2000, 2001, 2002 by Eugene H. Peterson. Used by permission of NavPress. All rights reserved. Represented by Tyndale House Publishers, Inc.

Scripture quotations labeled NASB are from the New American Standard Bible®

(NASB), copyright © 1960, 1962, 1963, 1968, 1971, 1972, 1973, 1975, 1977, 1995 by The Lockman Foundation. Used by permission. www.Lockman.org

Scripture quotations labeled NLT are from the Holy Bible, New Living Translation, copyright © 1996, 2004, 2007, 2013, 2015 by Tyndale House Foundation. Used by permission of Tyndale House Publishers, Inc., Carol Stream, Illinois 60188. All rights reserved.

Scripture quotations labeled NRSV are from the New Revised Standard Version of the Bible, copyright © 1989 National Council of the Churches of Christ in the United States of America. Used by permission. All rights reserved.

Scripture quotations labeled TPT are from The Passion Translation®. Copyright © 2017 by BroadStreet Publishing® Group, LLC. Used by permission. All rights reserved.

All text reprinted by permission of its respective author.

(in)courage is represented by Alive Literary Agency, www.aliveliterary.com.

In keeping with biblical principles of creation stewardship, Baker Publishing Group advocates the responsible use of our natural resources. As a member of the Green Press Initiative, our company uses recycled paper when possible. The text paper of this book is composed in part of post-consumer waste.

green press
INITIATIVE

20 21 22 23 24 25 26   7 6 5 4 3 2 1

For our (in)courage community.
Thank you for sharing your own stories of pain,
for praying for one another, and for embodying
what it means to "mourn with those who mourn"
(Romans 12:15). This one's for you.

introduction

None of us are immune to the burdens and pains of this life. Though we have a God who loves us, we all experience loss, hardship, and disappointment. And in the midst of it all, it might feel as though we're all alone, with no one to understand us, no one to guide us, no one to let us know they've been there too.

Sometimes, in those seasons of life that ache beyond words, we just want to hear that it's okay to not feel okay. We want to know we're not alone in this chasm of loneliness we stand in. We want to be held by arms that bear the scars of similar wounds.

In our most vulnerable moments, we need more than pithy statements that attempt to assure us that all will be well. Instead, we need one another's stories. Stories create a space for us to be—to be known, to be validated in our feelings and experiences, and to give us words to express what we might not have been able to say before. We can find ourselves and God again in one another's stories, opening the door to let hope come through once more.

We won't be able to understand why hard things happen in this world or in our lives, and that is okay. We can sit in the tension of that reality together. And not only do our suffering and pain connect us in our humanity, they also connect us to Christ, who bore it all on the cross. He held the tension between heaven's holiness and the world's brokenness, and though we all long for resurrection, we have a God who stayed in the tomb—in darkness, in death, in time suspended—before He rose again the third day.

And these are His words to us:

In this world you will have trouble. But take heart! I have overcome the world. (John 16:33)

Day 1

getting honest about depression and anxiety

> I will be with you
> when you pass through the waters,
> and when you pass through the rivers,
> they will not overwhelm you.
> You will not be scorched
> when you walk through the fire,
> and the flame will not burn you.
>
> Isaiah 43:2 CSB

I'm standing on a stage in front of a crowd of women. I see teenagers with side ponytails, sweet mamas in skinny jeans, and lovely silver-haired seniors. I wish for the chance to have coffee with them all, to hear their stories one by one. So I do what I consider to be second-best—I tell mine.

I come to the part about how we all have bullies in our lives. Mine hassled my elementary friends and me after school, until one day he called me a word none of us were supposed to utter under any circumstances. At this point I decided to take matters into my own hands. Although the quiet and gentle type, I promptly pushed him down—without causing injury or serious concern from any adult authorities—and sat on his back until he promised to repent of his bully ways. The audience laughs

9

at this, and I tell them I wish this was my only encounter with a bully. But I still fight them every day.

My grown-up bullies are anxiety and depression, two words we can be hesitant to say at church. Yet the psalmist freely confesses, "I am deeply depressed" (Ps. 42:6 CSB). Struggling with depression or anxiety doesn't mean we are spiritual failures, we've disappointed God, or we're not strong enough. This is what I have come to believe: we live in a fallen, broken world, and if we are in a battle, it simply means we are warriors.

I declare this to the women in the room, and after the session, one of the leaders says to me, "When you said those words, I could hear a collective sigh of relief." After I finish speaking, a line of women that stretches almost out the door forms in front of me, and one after another says either "Me too" or "My daughter struggles with depression and anxiety." If you're reading this and you or someone you love is in this battle, know you're not alone.

The hope in all this is that Jesus has promised us victory. I believe I will likely have to fight this battle as long as I'm on this spinning earth. But through a plan that includes every part of who I am—spiritual, emotional, social, physical, and mental—these days I'm winning more than I'm losing. I also have partners in the fight, including a counselor, a doctor, and good friends who speak truth to me on the days I can't remember it. (When people ask me what to do next about their depression and anxiety, I always recommend starting with a trustworthy biblical counselor.)

What we don't talk about, what we keep secret, where we let shame and guilt take hold are the places in our lives where we remain defeated and unhealed. So I'm speaking publicly about this struggle with you too.

Depression and anxiety are part of my life, but they're not the boss of me. They're also not my identity. I'm strong, brave, and loved. I'm a daughter of God who has been promised victory. So are you. There is no shame in being a warrior. Fight on.

PRAYER

Lord, like the psalmist, I long to freely confess my truth. I am deeply depressed. Yet even as I speak those words, the next to fly out of my mouth is the truth that as I fight, I am a warrior, and in that there is no shame. Thank You, Lord, for the victory of speaking up, of not keeping secrets, of healing and identity. Help me live into mine. Amen.

Day 2

when you feel like you take up too much space

See what great love the Father has lavished on us, that we should be called children of God! And that is what we are!

1 John 3:1

I love traveling. I love airports too. Flying, though? I hate flying.

See, I'm overweight. And while that fact is always present in my thoughts, never am I more aware of my extra pounds than when I fly. I hate flying because I take up too much space.

If I have the choice, I always choose an aisle seat. I hold my breath and suck in my gut and pray that the seatbelt will latch. And then I spend the next few hours squeezing my legs together and digging my elbows into my sides as I try to avoid taking up any extra space—in the aisle, in the seats, in the air.

My scrunched-up and sucked-in body language, along with my apologetic glances and occasional "sorrys" after the inevitable bumps and elbow rubs, is one big apology.

I'm sorry for taking up too much space.

I'm sorry for being too big.

I'm sorry for being in the way.

I'm sorry I'm kind of sweaty from speed-walking to the gate.

I'm sorry I reached over you to turn on my fan.

I'm sorry my leg bumped your leg.

I'm sorry I'm in the way.

I'm sorry you have to sit by me.

Maybe you fit just fine in an airplane seat. Maybe it's something else that makes you hunch your shoulders and stare at the ground with red cheeks, apologizing for part of who you are, for just being yourself.

Are you clumsy? Perpetually late? Awkward? Too talkative? Too loud? Too quiet? Too sarcastic? Too much? Too real? *Too you?*

No you aren't. You are wonderful. You are loved. And when God looks at His creation (that's you! and me!), He says, "It is very good." Regardless of how anyone else sees us, we are God's workmanship and masterpiece—and He lavishes His love on us.

If you're tempted to apologize for who you are or how you are, please don't. Remember that you have a right to be here, to take up space—in a conversation, on the airplane, in the grocery store aisle, at the moms group, in the world. And no matter how much space you take up or how you take up that space, you are welcome and wanted and loved.

PRAYER

Thank You, Lord, for being a safe place where I am called good, where I take up just the right amount of space, where I am seen and loved and welcome to be who I am, how I am, just as I am. Even saying that calms my heart and lets me breathe deeper. Give me the strength to truly recognize that no matter how anyone else sees me, I am God's workmanship and masterpiece, and I am loved. Amen.

Day 3

holding on to God's presence when you've had enough

> Then he lay down under the bush and fell asleep.
>
> All at once an angel touched him and said, "Get up and eat." He looked around, and there by his head was some bread baked over hot coals, and a jar of water. He ate and drank and then lay down again.
>
> The angel of the LORD came back a second time and touched him and said, "Get up and eat, for the journey is too much for you."
>
> 1 Kings 19:5–7

I used to believe that determination and hard work were my greatest strengths. Whether in family, ministry, career, or health, there was no challenge I couldn't conquer, no problem I couldn't solve. I come from a long line of copper miners, men and women who weren't afraid to roll up their sleeves and get dirty. I took great pride in my fearless work ethic, anxious to prove to the world—and to God Himself—that I wasn't wasting my skin.

But then a long stretch of consecutive losses sapped my strength. Betrayal, divorce, single motherhood, stepfamily, adoption, and three bouts of head and neck cancer. In the span of a decade, my sleeve-rolling self collapsed, exhausted.

I couldn't work, let alone work hard. Most mornings I struggled to wake up and face another day. When would the struggle end? When would God deliver relief? I had no more drive or determination.

That's when my silly pride turned to shame. What was wrong with me? Why couldn't I snap out of it? Why was I struggling so hard to put one foot in front of the other? The lies in my head told me that if I had enough faith I wouldn't be in this situation. "God will never give you more than you can handle," they whispered. And I believed them.

Until I remembered the story of Elijah.

Elijah was God's prophet during a time when God wasn't all that popular with ordinary people. Righteous and hard-working, Elijah followed God with fierce determination. He wasn't afraid of rejection or resistance, and he dove into danger again and again for the sake of God's name and glory.

But then the wicked King Ahab and Queen Jezebel put out a bounty on Elijah's life. Anxious to avoid death and disillusioned by God's lack of intervention, Elijah ran as far and fast as he could. Discouraged, he collapsed under a bush and begged God for relief:

> "I have had enough, Lord," he said. "Take my life; I am no better than my ancestors." (1 Kings 19:4)

When I read Elijah's words, my battered soul exhaled. Elijah was a good man who loved God. And yet life circumstances wore him down. He'd had enough, and he told God about it.

But the best part of Elijah's story? How God responded:

> All at once an angel touched him and said, "Get up and eat." He looked around, and there by his head was some bread baked over hot coals, and a jar of water. He ate and drank and then lay down again.
>
> The angel of the Lord came back a second time and touched him and said, "Get up and eat, for the journey is too much for you." (1 Kings 19:5–7)

For the journey is too much for you.

I might've read those words a dozen times. *Yes!* I wanted to shout. More often than not, the journey is too much for me. But rather than rebuke me or shame me for it, God meets me in it, curled up and buried by the weariness of life.

No matter the weariness that is taking you under, there is a God who meets you there. He is not surprised by your weakness, nor is He turned off by it. Instead, He longs to comfort you in it. Thus He touches you, feeds you, and gives you exactly what you need today to help you heal and rest for tomorrow.

PRAYER

God, I have had enough. From unending struggle to shame and back to struggle again . . . I'm done. I am begging You for relief. I am exhausted, and I need You. The journey is too much. So meet me right here, Lord. Take my hand, comfort me, feed me, and bring me exactly what I need today to help me heal and rest for tomorrow. Amen.

I'm strong, brave, and loved.

I'm a daughter of God
who has been promised victory.
So are you.
There is no shame
in being a warrior.
Fight on.

—HOLLEY GERTH

the foolishness of Christ

For the message of the cross is foolishness to those who are perishing, but to us who are being saved it is the power of God. For it is written:

> "I will destroy the wisdom of the wise;
>   the intelligence of the intelligent I will frustrate."

Where is the wise person? Where is the teacher of the law? Where is the philosopher of this age? Has not God made foolish the wisdom of the world? For since in the wisdom of God the world through its wisdom did not know him, God was pleased through the foolishness of what was preached to save those who believe. Jews demand signs and Greeks look for wisdom, but we preach Christ crucified: a stumbling block to Jews and foolishness to Gentiles, but to those whom God has called, both Jews and Greeks, Christ the power of God and the wisdom of God. For the foolishness of God is wiser than human wisdom, and the weakness of God is stronger than human strength.

1 Corinthians 1:18–25

Identity is such a fragile thing; we look for our significance in a million wayward places. We're swayed by those we assume have it all together—who have the perfect body or ministry or children or marriage or job. The perfect life.

I'm the girl who loved words and collected them like bread-crumbs to find her way home, the woman who let her story unfurl in the hand of God and tried her best to believe her weakness didn't disqualify her from being loved.

I have no credentials to speak of. I'm a high school dropout who got her GED. I have seventeen teeth left. I have chronic and mental illness. I have nothing to commend me.

I've spent my life in constant need of a Redeemer. I write from the threshing floor, but God continues to lift my head.

I want to pretend I'm not weak. But surviving bipolar disorder means my mind often betrays me. Sometimes my thoughts are jumbled, sometimes words don't come. They're thick and clunky, and I suffocate under the swell of them as I try to push them into the world. Sometimes my hands tremble and my heart shakes from the medications I'm on. I am ill. My body betrays me in a thousand different ways.

I wonder if I'm strong enough to live the life God has called me to.

This is my thorn. I am pierced among the beautiful and bloom-ing perennials, and despite my pleas, God chose for it to remain. Can I still flourish if I am never healed? Can I flourish if all I do is struggle? If around every corner is another detour, another devastation? But the Bible says, "The message of the cross is foolishness to those who are perishing, but to us who are being saved it is the power of God."

People who've yet to know Jesus look at my life and wonder how I claim a good and loving God. It is foolish naiveté to them. But to me, who is being saved, it is the power that keeps me moving forward with confidence.

I count myself among the foolishness of God, the ridiculous-ness of the cross.

The message of Christ crucified is ridiculous mercy. I've done nothing to earn God's tender mercy. I lack strength, but I have come to know that the abundant grace of God is all I need.

PRAYER

Lord, thank You for Your ridiculous mercy, Your foolish grace, Your unbelievable love. And thank You for Your strength. Help me to claim Your goodness from the depths of despair and the darkest of days, and thank You for saving me from them both. In Your power and fullness, amen.

GRACE P. CHO

seen by God in the loneliness of marriage

She gave this name to the Lord who spoke to her: "You are the God who sees me," for she said, "I have now seen the One who sees me."

Genesis 16:13

Life changes I hadn't seen coming knocked the wind out of me, and I'm short of breath, trying to make sense of the misunderstandings and buried resentments, straining to imagine a future where things don't hurt so much between my husband and me.

The changes have exposed the complicated knots that have formed over the course of our marriage from the lack of clear communication and intentional efforts to know one another, and I stand in a sea of bitterness and rage, anger and unforgiveness, resentment and a faltering faith that things will get better.

I wonder how two people so different from each other can make it work. How do we find a way through the tangle of differences that personality, family background, communication style, and love languages create?

I'm desperate to be known, to be heard, to have the burden shared, but I know it's not easy for others to enter into pain. I see the discomfort on my friends' faces when I open the door to my unending crisis and see them looking around at the mess, not sure what to say. They try to offer suggestions for why it might be. They ask pertinent and helpful—though tiring—questions. They try to comfort me with "at least" statements, wanting to tether me to the silver lining, but instead of feeling known, I feel even more unseen, nearly invisible.

The unresolved tensions in my life are too heavy to bear, so I close the door to my mess, letting my friends off the hook and comforting them by saying that things will get better for me.

The vulnerability hangover and the weight of holding everyone else's discomfort make me want to hide in a little corner and curl up like a child. I pull a blanket of silence around me, and in this quiet place I wrestle with God, with the gospel, with what it means to love and die in this commitment of marriage. I cry out and beg, "Do *You* see me, God?" and I get wrecked by His gentle response of love, by His holding me like no one else can.

I wish the years of hurt could be touched and healed by God with the zap of a lightning bolt. I wish I could labor through the pain with an epidural and come to a place of relief as quickly as others would like me to, as quickly as *I* would like to. But is resurrection even possible when what needs to die hasn't finished dying yet?

Like the browning and falling of leaves in autumn, there's a process to the dying, and it will not be rushed. Everything that has been in our marriage is being put through the fire, and what needs to die must die for new life to eventually be brought forth.

And is this not the way of Christ? Dying is part of life in Him. It was the way He chose to bridge the gap between us, the way He chose to love us.

He understands this way of death and the process of becoming, and He does not need the mess to be cleaned up before He will sit with us. Instead, He walks with us in the dark, guiding us to the light of hope, and He assures us along the way, "I see you, I know you, and I love you."

PRAYER

God, even when it seems that no one can or wants to understand my pain, You already know. You have been in that dark place before. You understand the wait, the longing, and the breakthrough that new life can bring, so I pray the same for this hard place in marriage when things feel hopeless and so lonely. Be with me, and I pray for the strength to keep going. Amen.

Day 6

from the soil of dead dreams

Build homes, and plan to stay. Plant gardens, and eat the food they produce. . . . And work for the peace and prosperity of the city where I sent you into exile. Pray to the LORD for it, for its welfare will determine your welfare.

Jeremiah 29:5, 7 NLT

We were so sure about the call to ministry on our lives even before we got married. It was what connected us as a couple, the thing that took us from one address and assignment to another, and eventually to Germany together. Germany was one of our last stops, the last clear call we heard from God, our last hope to see if something in ministry might actually work out for us in the long haul. But what had once felt like the greatest purpose of our lives—both as individuals and as a couple—started to feel like wearing clothes in the wrong size. We wrestled to make them fit, constantly adjusting and readjusting the way we looked at the future.

After Germany, we moved back to the States, and after another year of full-time ministry, we left it. We stepped into a landscape of wilderness and silence. We began living lives we didn't imagine we would be living, in a place I never wanted to live in.

We clung to each other as we wrestled through the slow grief of our dreams dying. There were days of melancholy and longing, repeated prayers of pleading to be called back to what was, tearful nights, and quiet, lonely dinners. The days piled up one after another, seemingly void of purpose. The nagging feeling that we were doing something wrong, or that we ourselves were wrong and not good enough to be in ministry, followed me around like an ugly shadow.

I wish I could say it became easier after a few rough months. But the death of anything never comes easy. And for years the grief of those dead dreams kept coming back without invitation. But we tended to the simple things right in front of us. We started noticing the neighbors around us. We moved toward the ones we didn't choose, the ones chosen for us. These tiny things became our seeds. We watered them with tears of grief, the ache of discontent, and slivers of hope. And over time our tiny, imperfect offering of dreams come undone became a beautiful garden. It was in this garden that I began to learn how to be still and to receive. This unexpected garden began to nourish us.

I see now what I couldn't see ten years ago: the death of my dream was not the death of God's dreams for me.

PRAYER

God, this doesn't look like I thought it would, and it's breaking my heart. Yet I'm in a place of learning how to be still and how to receive, and my hands are open to Your plan. Nourish me in this unexpected garden and help me see that the death of this dream is not the death of Your dreams for me. Amen.

Day 7

i am counted

Aren't five sparrows sold for two pennies? Yet not one of them is forgotten in God's sight. Indeed, the hairs of your head are all counted. Don't be afraid; you are worth more than many sparrows.

Luke 12:6–7 CSB

After three years of trying, testing, waiting, crying, bargaining, accepting . . . two blue lines.

The tiny secret unfurling inside of me brought so much joy, we thought we'd burst.

And then eleven weeks later, it ended. Just as suddenly and shockingly as it had begun.

My first miscarriage was the greatest pain I'd experienced to date. The physical pain was crippling and terrifying, but it paled in comparison to my broken heart. I sobbed for days, the wound reopening fresh with each phone call to unknowing, still-excited family members. Each tiny sock and sweater tucked away again for someday. Each pregnant woman I saw at the grocery store, bellies full and round and alive.

At first the pain was palpable. I could feel it throbbing throughout my entire body. Slowly it dulled to more of a constant ache, accompanying me throughout my days, unseen by anyone else. Then it turned into a sharp twist in my gut, flaring up whenever I saw a pregnancy or birth announcement on Facebook. It became bitterness, an acid that choked me when I had thoughts like, *She doesn't deserve to have a baby—I do. Doesn't what I want matter? Don't I count?*

Just writing this brings me back.

That first miscarriage was almost ten years ago now. My second miscarriage was eight years ago. And while the pain isn't as sharp, it lingers.

A friend once told me that the pain of infertility and miscarriage never goes away, even after or if you have children. She was absolutely right. There's no expiration on grief; it just changes.

About a year later, we did have a baby. That pregnancy was full of anxiety for me, worry creeping around every corner and discoloring my joy. That crept into my new motherhood too, making me double-check the thermostat to make sure my baby wasn't too hot, sneak into his room and place my hand under his nose to make sure he was breathing, drive like a driver's ed teacher to make sure we weren't in an accident.

I wanted all the control because nothing about becoming a mother had been within my control.

There was, for me, only fear and distrust and an intense feeling of being overlooked. Unseen. Discounted.

Which is not what God says we are.

God promises that even in our pain, we are seen. We count. We matter to Him. God doesn't overlook us. When I came out of the initial fog of grief, I turned to today's Scripture passage and begged God to make it stick in my soul. If He remembered and cared for birds (a creature I myself do not much care for), how much more would He remember and care about me?

So much more.

I begged and He answered, and so daily, faithfully, I placed my own self and all the babies I was longing for in His hands. I knew I was seen. I knew I mattered. I knew that I counted to Him. Honestly, it didn't fix the pain, but it eased some of the sorrow.

And when my three babies were born, I knew every single hair on their heads had also been counted.

PRAYER

God, how can it be that I am not overlooked? When everything I've been longing for, hoping for, banking on is passing me by? I don't understand it, yet You've promised that I matter more to You than the birds You remember. You've said You counted the hairs on my head. You've said that I am seen. So today, even for just this moment, I'm trusting You and sighing with relief at the gift of being remembered. And for this moment, maybe for this day, that will ease some of the sorrow. Thank You for seeing me, caring for me, loving me. Amen.

Day 8

on the outside looking in

After this, I'm coming back;
  I'll rebuild David's ruined house;
I'll put all the pieces together again;
  I'll make it look like new
So outsiders who seek will find,
  so they'll have a place to come to.

Acts 15:15–16 MSG

I sat at the restaurant table with two other women, one whose friendship I'd delighted in for some time and the other whom I looked forward to getting to know better. Both women had known each other for years—long before either one had met me. Still, our trio's conversation flowed easily, and I thought we were all having a bang-up time.

Eventually the conversation turned toward a concert the other two were attending together. Given the shared history of these two women, I didn't expect an invite (although I wouldn't have minded one). But as they talked on and on *and on* about their plans right there over our three plates of enchiladas, I also didn't expect to feel so awkward . . . like the quintessential third wheel.

They do realize I'm still sitting here, don't they? I thought. I wanted to ask the question out loud, but instead I sighed and took my phone out of my purse. As I scrolled through a few Instagram pics, I thought of a similar scenario my twin sons had told me

29

about a few weeks before. As they relayed it, one of the boys at their youth group meeting proceeded to invite every same-aged kid to his birthday party—that is, everyone but the two of them.

We've all been there, haven't we? I tell ya, we can be grown up on the outside and still feel very much like a schoolkid on the inside. We've felt left out in obvious ways, like when we wait for the invite that never comes. We've felt left out in less obvious ways as well, like when that person you really admire unfollows you on social media. Whatever being on the outside looks like for you, it feels like you lost a measure of your belonging, and it hurts like the dickens.

When this kind of thing happens to me, two things help banish those hurtful feelings that try to boss me into believing I don't belong—and never will.

First of all, we are each called to pay attention to and invest our time in the people and places God directs us to. As hard as it is to accept, sometimes you and I are going to fall outside another's investment. If we're honest, we have to admit there are people and places that fall outside our own investments too. In recognition of this fact, I pray we each have the wisdom and sensitivity to choose behavior that doesn't overtly hurt another. But because most of us—all of us—have failed to do that before, each of us can extend grace to another when she does the same. Each of us can remember, "Generally speaking, this isn't about what's wrong with me. This is about her doing what's right for her and God's priorities for her."

Second, as my friend Salena says, sometimes rejection is God's protection against what isn't in our best interest. Rejection is never fun, but it is a reality that God allows. As hard as it is to believe in the moment, God's provision and grace can look like being on the outside of where we want to be on the inside.

By turning our backs on pride and our faces toward trust in God, let us remember that there's always room at the table God chooses for us. As we pray for God to show us where that is—and where we belong—let us not be on the outside looking in.

Let us be on the outside looking up.

PRAYER

Not belonging is an awful feeling, Lord—one that You understand. It's awkward and disappointing and embarrassing, and the rejection that follows is just as painful. Walk me through these feelings with my face turned toward trust in You. Remind me, in Your faithful love, that there is always room at the table You've chosen for me. Help me see Your provision and grace from the outside of where I want to be. Amen.

What if God's plan
for us is not to be more busy
but to be more loved?
Hear God whisper to you today,

You are beautiful to Me.
Come away with Me and rest a while.

Be kind to yourself and find a place
for your weary soul to rest
in His irrevocable love for you.

—BONNIE GRAY

it's okay to set and keep boundaries

Like a city whose walls are broken through
is a person who lacks self-control.

Proverbs 25:28

A long time ago, I was wounded deeply and repeatedly by some-one in my life. A spiritual director advised me to set up boundaries to protect my heart and mind. As a result, I essentially broke off connection with this person. It was heartbreaking and hard.

But I had moved on—or at least I thought so.

Trouble was, I would keep tabs and check in by seeing what this person was up to on social media. If I overheard the person's name in conversation, I would try to gather information.

I hadn't really moved on at all, and instead of protecting the boundary, the extra intel I was gathering only served to deepen the wound.

For a variety of reasons, it can be difficult for us to protect our boundaries. Sometimes we are hoping that there's a way to restore what was broken. Other times we are simply curious.

Have you found yourself in the same position I was in? Have you set up appropriate boundaries in your life, only to find yourself breaching them from time to time in ways that seem harmless?

God has something interesting to say to us in Proverbs 25:28 about boundaries: "Like a city whose walls are broken through is a person who lacks self-control."

That verse convicts me when I read it. I know that when I am keeping tabs, I lack self-control. That lack of self-control creates weak places in boundaries that had been set previously. However, we are not powerless to this temptation. Self-control is within our grasp because of the Holy Spirit and the fruit He grows in us (see Gal. 5:22–23). Through the Holy Spirit, we can gain mastery over our temptations, so we can keep those boundary walls standing strong.

It really is okay to set and keep boundaries. Good boundaries help you heal. They increase your ability to tend the healthy relationships in your life because you aren't being consumed with the toxicity that needs to stay behind the wall you set up.

For my part, someday perhaps God will restore that fractured relationship. Perhaps.

But if not, I will choose to turn my eyes and attention to the people and things that heal, not hurt. And I hope you have the courage to do the same.

PRAYER

This is a hard one, Lord. I need help with boundaries, with self-control, with mastering the lure of "just checking" on that one person's Instagram feed. I know those boundaries will help heal my heart, but it's so tempting to break right through them. So I trust You, Lord, and I trust Your plan for this broken relationship. Give me strength to uphold the boundaries I need in order to tend the healthy relationships in my life and to turn my eyes and attention to that which heals. Amen.

Day 10

experiencing glory
in our grief

Then Jesus said, "Did I not tell you that if you believe, you will see the glory of God?"

John 11:40

I always feel it at the end of the summer when my kids go back to school. It's a slow ache deep in my bones that shows up unannounced. A sadness triggered in different ways by a place, a moment, a feeling that reminds me of my husband's final days on earth. This is the season of grief.

Ericlee soared to heaven on September 9, 2014. Before I'm even aware of the date on the calendar, my body is telling me—it's time. I remember when the cancer spread from the tumor on his hip to his lymph nodes and lungs. His suffering was like torture to me.

That was the year I chose *glory* as my word theme. I had no idea I would experience such grief and so many glimpses of God's glory. Glory is the very essence of God. It's who He is. It's what makes Him unique. It's what gives us greater understanding of His kingdom.

In John 11, Jesus goes to the home of his dear friends Mary and Martha. Their brother Lazarus has just died. The two women are deeply grieving. Both believed Jesus could have healed Lazarus, but He arrives four days after Lazarus's death.

35

Jesus does two notable things. First, He takes time to grieve with His friends. John 11:35 simply says, "Jesus wept." These words have been especially meaningful to me. Jesus knew the miracle that was to come for Lazarus. He knew the miracle that would unfold in my life too, but He still took time to empathize. He proved Himself a God of comfort who cares about each one of us in a very personal way. We are often quick to brush aside or swallow our grief, but our Savior makes space for it.

Then Jesus goes to the tomb with Martha and commands that the stone be removed from its entrance. In John 11:39, Martha points out that Lazarus's body has already been there for four days, and there's probably an overwhelming odor. (I love that she's thinking about the stench when Jesus is preparing for the miracle.)

Jesus challenges her with this poignant question: "Did I not tell you that if you believed you would see the glory of God?" He used this question to reach me in my circumstances as well. He challenged me to look for His glory in my husband's sickness and death.

Here's what I learned: Jesus is never late. Believe me, as the days passed during my husband's cancer journey, I often felt like Jesus was late. I wrestled with why He allowed this cancer. I questioned why my husband had to suffer so much. I struggled to comprehend how taking away the daddy of my three daughters could actually bring God glory.

But Jesus is never late. Martha knew it. I knew it. And the story was just unfolding. Jesus raised Lazarus from the grave, and many Jews came to believe in Him as the Son of God. Although my husband was not raised from the dead on earth, I believe he now has a new body in heaven.

God continues to write this resurrection story. Each year as we celebrate my husband's heaven-iversary, God continues to surprise me with His faithfulness. I see His glory dancing in the colors of every sunset, in the provision for our medical bills, in the way He gives me courage to preach and share this message of hope. We still grieve the loss of Ericlee. We long for heaven.

We've also learned that we need to make space for both the grief and the glory. God will meet us in both.

PRAYER

I have so many questions, Lord. I don't understand the why behind any of my grief, especially when it comes to You. Why the suffering? Why death? Why are You not showing up on time? *Yet even as I question, I know You are good, and I know there is glory to be seen even in this despair. Help me make space for the grief and the glory, knowing that You will meet me in both. Amen.*

Day 11

not designed for division

> I have given them the glory you have given me, so that they may be one as we are one. I am in them and you are in me, so that they may be made completely one, that the world may know you have sent me and have loved them as you have loved me.
>
> John 17:22-23 CSB

On the eve of His death, Jesus had not yet seen us, His people, reconcile our unified identity. He acknowledged the corrupt world order in which we exist—where people groups are in discord, where women are devalued, and where religious abuse exploits the most vulnerable. In His lament, Jesus turns to the Father and pours out His last and longest recorded prayer. Jesus wields His words to paint the picture of unity between God and us. Like a talented craftsman, Jesus chisels a world aligned with His Father's heart for unity with humanity. In this complete unity, He prays, the world will know God's love.

I am black. My husband is white. While in college, our friendship blossomed as we uprooted deeply entrenched racial, social, and cultural divides to integrate a church. So it feels a little unfitting to classify the life we have created with each other as an "interracial marriage." We are two souls committed to each other just as any other married couple. We have three children. Like all humans, our children were wholly and holy crafted in their mother's womb. They are not hybrids or "mixed" like two paint colors. In our home, we thrive in the unity Jesus imagined and longed for—unity with God and with one another.

Aligned with Jesus's prayer, we work to dismantle constructs that feed a society hinged on division. We celebrate the beauty of our various skin tones and our blend of ethnic and cultural backgrounds. We tell the truth about the injustices of race and racism in order to foster healing from its lies.

But outside of our home, the world is different. For some people, the unity in our family threatens their comfort with division and a broken humanity. To those who feel threatened, we are not a reflection of the love Jesus prayed for but a racial inconvenience. Our love challenges their preconceived belief that humanity was designed to be divided.

So, sadly, I am at times overlooked and invisible to white women who find it difficult to see me as a valuable treasure to my husband. I have been called terrible names by black men who don't approve of me being with my husband. Some people think our children aren't black enough. Others think our children are misfits because they aren't white enough. One neighbor took the liberty of informing our neighborhood that he did not approve of our "interracial marriage." But he was not to be outdone by a fellow parishioner, who shared the same sentiment at our multiethnic church.

As a wife and mom, I am devastated when society's commitment to division and complacency about race and racism collide with our family's expressed unity and love. Perhaps this was how Jesus felt on the eve of His crucifixion as He saw humanity wallowing in a false reality. Maybe He saw us reflecting a corrupt, fear-filled, divided world, knowing that we were meant for more. He cried out to the Father as He saw us sitting comfortably in a fractured state but knew that we could be whole, in unity with the Father and with one another.

Do we lament and long for unity as Jesus did? Do we ache with the weightiness of His prayer that's still in the process of being answered? When we do, we are in line with Jesus and carry the burden He felt as well. Unity was Jesus's vision for us, and when it seems like too much to even hope for it, let's do as He did and go to the Father. Let's keep showing up and asking in prayer that we become united in His love.

PRAYER

Lord, my heart feels as fractured as our world. I am crying out for unity in our homes, in our communities, in our countries, in our world. This still-in-the-process-of-being-answered prayer is a weighty burden, one that You carried first. And as You modeled, I now mimic: Father, may we be one. Amen.

Day 12

unraveling anxiety

Let us then with confidence draw near to the throne of grace, that we may receive mercy and find grace to help in time of need.

Hebrews 4:16 ESV

It was an ordinary Tuesday morning. I was engrossed in work at my kitchen desk when my husband decided to make lemon bars.

Glass bakeware clinked together as Chris pulled dishes from the cupboard. I leaned closer to my computer. Parchment paper ripped across the jagged metal line. I reread an email. Chris carefully lined the pan with waxy paper. Every crinkle sent a shock wave of irritation up my spine. Eggs cracked. The metal whisk bounced.

I tried to fill my heavy lungs.

Then he started to zest. Every time the lemon scraped the length of the grater, my insides cringed.

This is stupid, I told myself. *Get a grip.*

But I couldn't get a grip. I was unraveling. Fat tears slid down my cheeks.

"What's wrong?" my husband asked.

I shrugged my shoulders. "I don't know. The noise is just too much for me right now."

I walked into the bathroom, shut the door, and cried.

I wasn't worried or upset about anything specific, which was the most frustrating thing about my anxiety. If I couldn't

41

explain the *why* of what I was feeling, it seemed invalid to feel it.

I gasped for air and prayed for a way to make sense of my mess.

Eventually my breathing slowed. A new thought emerged. I walked back into the kitchen.

"Hey, I think I can help us understand my reaction," I began. "When someone has a bad toothache, normal eating is suddenly extremely painful. The food isn't the problem. It's touching the exposed or damaged nerve that produces a visceral reaction you can't control. This is what anxiety is like. Making lemon bars isn't the issue. My anxiety is like raw nerves. When certain noises touch those nerves, my system is overwhelmed. My body deals with it through tears."

I'm not sure if this made things clearer to my husband, but it helped me. Giving voice to our experience can help unravel the tangle of shame we're living in.

Anxiety is real. And it's not always synonymous with fear-driven worry. Anxiety can also be a mental health disorder. We don't try to downplay a screaming toothache or criticize ourselves for low iron. We acknowledge the problem. We take steps to get better.

I'm thankful for God's mercy in using lemon zest to help me understand my brokenness. My anxiety has ebbed for now. But when it flares again, I will be ready to admit it, seek help, and be gentle with myself.

PRAYER

I need You, Lord, right now. This is me, crawling to Your throne of grace, seeking mercy and help. I need deep breaths and deep love. Help me understand my brokenness, help me lean into You and ask for what I need in times of anxiety, and help me be gentle with myself. You've loved me with a gentle strength, and that's what I need now. Amen.

Day 13

a different kind of freedom

God saw all that he had made, and it was very good. And there was evening, and there was morning—the sixth day.

Genesis 1:31

In my small hometown, the Fourth of July was a big deal— baby parades, talent shows, carnival games, soft pretzels, and fireworks that ended with a sparkling American flag while the national anthem blared over the park loudspeakers.

The real high point came at dusk with the Queen of the Candles Pageant.

Each spring a dozen high school senior girls were chosen by secret ballot. On the Fourth of July, the girl with the most votes was proclaimed Queen of the Candles. Thousands of candles were lit along the stone-lined stream that ran through the park as the queen remained onstage, beaming. All around her stood her court, the other eleven girls, their eyes wet with unshed tears.

Chosen but not crowned. Pretty but not pretty enough.

I watched the pageant unfold every summer of my childhood and imagined myself in a long gown, wavy hair piled on my head. Deep down I knew I wasn't queen material, but maybe I could be part of her court? Just *one* of the twelve?

My hopes began to fade as the seasons passed and reality set in. By my senior year, I knew the truth. I was popular with the girls in my class because I was funny and friendly, but I would *not* be strolling across the amphitheater stage on the Fourth of July. No way.

As voting day approached, my father assured me, "Don't worry. You'll be in the pageant."

I knew better. I didn't have the right hair, the right shape, the right look. When a dozen of my smiling friends lit their candles on stage that hot summer night, I was the one fighting tears.

Because of that disappointment and many more like it, I spent the next ten years desperately trying to find a man who would call me beautiful. (The sad truth? Some guys will call a woman *anything* just to get her in bed.) It was a long, lost decade full of poor choices and lame excuses.

Then I discovered what *beautiful* really means.

After years of feeling *less than*, I met a God who called me *more than*.

A God who "rewards those who earnestly seek him" (Heb. 11:6).

A God who "crowns the humble with victory" (Ps. 149:4).

A God who "saw all that he had made" and called it "very good" (Gen. 1:31).

In Him, I found a different kind of freedom—the freedom to stop worrying about whether or not people love me and simply love *them*. The freedom to accept whatever God gave me in the way He created me to live for His glory. The freedom to stand in front of a mirror and say, "Ta-da!"

I've also learned what makes us beautiful to God: the light in our eyes, the glow on our faces, and the warmth of our words.

Just as a candle captures our attention when it's lit, a woman whose eyes shine with Christ's love stands out in a crowd. She knows "the eye is the lamp of the body" (Matt. 6:22) and the Holy Spirit is her light source.

A radiant complexion? Also an inside job. As we all "with unveiled faces contemplate the Lord's glory," we are "transformed into his image with ever-increasing glory, which comes from the Lord, who is the Spirit" (2 Cor. 3:18).

And those warm words, that tender voice? They demonstrate "the unfading beauty of a gentle and quiet spirit, which is of great worth in God's sight" (1 Pet. 3:4).

Rest, knowing you were chosen and "loved by God" (1 Thess. 1:4)—the One who calls you beautiful and means it.

PRAYER

God, from the very beginning, even before You created the world, You considered me, and when You made me, You called me very good. Nothing can change that. When the standards of the world and my inner critic tell me otherwise, help me to remember the truth and to recognize that the beauty I see in You resides in me as well. Amen.

Day 14

for those who feel like they are dying on the inside

> He who was seated on the throne said, "I am making every-
> thing new!" Then he said, "Write this down, for these words
> are trustworthy and true."
>
> Revelation 21:5

Maybe you're dying a little bit on the inside. Every day there are little pieces of your soul crumbling and crying and dying. Maybe you're between the loads of laundry and feel stuck in this mundane rut of a routine. Maybe it's the commuter lane at rush hour that's got you bent over the steering wheel thinking, "I just can't do this anymore. I'm no one's rat, and I just can't take this mind-numbing race anymore."

Maybe your daughter has leukemia, and your heart really is dying every single day you lie next to her on a hospital bed. Maybe your mom died when she turned forty-two, and now you're only two years shy of that age. Maybe it's your marriage that has died, all those wedding vows crumbled like old plaster into dust gathering on photo albums. Maybe you haven't seen your son in a month, and he's stopped returning your calls, stopped talking to you, stopped letting you into his life.

Maybe your insides hurt so badly that you can't believe no one notices. Maybe your soul is bloody and messy and desperately lonely, and you just need to know you're not alone.

We have a faith that says we are all one body and that if one part aches, the rest of the body does as well (Rom. 12). If one part bleeds, the whole body suffers that blood loss. If one part is dying, the whole body must face death—or fight it.

I've lived enough of this life broken and loved enough friends through their own cracks to know that redeemed isn't the same as fixed and that holes can still ache when we're whole again. Death, divorce, loss, heartbreak—admitting them doesn't make us immune, nor does it cancel the loss or restore what's missing.

But sometimes saying it out loud is an invitation to the God who already knows to lay Himself down in our rips and tears and holds us together—often through the arms of our friends, through the people who have heard us whisper, "I'm not fine."

So it's time to be brave and tell someone how you feel. It's time to let someone into your secret insides. Because while it can be excruciating to admit our un-fine moments, it's in those moments that people can actually get to us to help us. We need each other. Though people can let you down and will likely hurt you sometimes, they will also laugh with you over the everyday bits and pieces that make us real.

It's our calling as Jesus followers to sit down beside each other as we crumple in the valley of the shadow of death. Today, when you feel like you're dying inside, know that you're not alone.

PRAYER

Lord, sometimes it's scary and vulnerable to even tell You that I'm not okay. But there is no safer place to come broken and empty and exhausted than Your presence. Here I am, with all the brokenness that lives inside me and around me. Thank You for being able to hold it all and for cherishing my tears. My sorrows are not lost on You, and the gift of that is not lost on me. Sit with me, Lord, right here beside me as I fall apart. May Your Spirit intercede for me when I simply don't have the words. In Your name, amen.

counseling is saving my life

And you will know the truth, and the truth will set you free.

John 8:32 NLT

Counseling is saving my life.

Jesus saved it first, but counseling saves it regularly.

I sit in Marie's office every other week. I get the same sick feeling in the pit of my stomach each time I sit on that cushy blue couch. I think the sick feeling is called courage.

Marie says the same thing to me whenever we meet. "Thank you for coming. I'm so glad you're here."

With a wavering voice, unsure if I actually believe myself, I reply, "Me too."

Most of the time I don't want to go. Most of the time I am riddled with anxiety the night before my appointment. Most of the time I have to force my suddenly iron legs up the wooden staircase to the front door. Most of the time I'd rather go to bed or eat Doritos instead of sitting across from Marie. But most of the time I choose to go anyway. Like so many other hard, healing things, counseling takes courage.

I think courage often looks like a tiny step forward instead of a leap.

Whenever my appointment comes, I wrestle with the tension of not wanting to go. But each time I choose to show up, I feel

49

grateful for the space Marie offers—space to grieve, to cuss, and to hear the voice of God.

I want to be free from the shame I drag around with me each day. And along with the kindness of God, this counseling center has given me a place to drop my shame. Sometimes I pick it up again, but Jesus and Marie always offer me a chance to put it back down.

Jesus came to give us life and life to the full. He said, "The truth will set you free." I earnestly believe God wants us to be honest with the stories we've been given. I think honesty first looks like admitting the truth to yourself, and then admitting the truth to a trusted person. For me, that person is my counselor.

We aren't meant to drag shame around with us like a dirty, wet blanket. We are meant to be people of the light, to walk in freedom. I pray you find a safe place to honestly tell the truth about your story—with a trusted friend or counselor.

Have courage, friend. You've got Jesus, who is the Truth.

And the Truth will set you free.

PRAYER

God, guide me to that which brings life and freedom in Your truth. Give me courage to accept the avenues through which that life and freedom come, be it counseling, medication, or honesty. I'll need grace for the setbacks that are bound to show up, but I promise to show up too. Amen.

Day 16

when sadness sits on your lap

> Even when I go through the darkest valley,
> I fear no danger,
> for you are with me;
> your rod and your staff—they comfort me.
>
> Psalm 23:4 CSB

It had been a hard day and an even harder night. I was overwhelmed with grief and uncertainty and needed to leave my house. I texted my best friend.

> Can I come over after the kids go to bed?

Her reply instantly appeared on my screen.

> Of course.

I took a deep breath, knowing that sitting with her would help me to feel better.

The past months had been some of the most difficult of my life. Pain, sadness, and loneliness were my constant companions. Only a few trusted friends knew my story, and she was one of them.

A few hours later I pulled into her driveway, her porch lights greeting me first. Her house that night was a quiet, safe sanctuary.

51

Her presence felt the same. Our friendship had been marked by the sorrows that come with life. It had always been that in the hardest times, we were knit together tighter.

She embraced me as soon as I walked in the door. We moved to her sitting room, its two large leather chairs awaiting us. For the next two hours I sat in one of those chairs, sobbing, talking, and sobbing some more. The tissue box grew emptier and the mound of wet tissue grew taller on the table beside me. My friend sat with me, intently listening, offering kindness and compassion.

At one point, overcome with her own sadness, she got out of her chair and climbed into my lap. It was a purposeful act of unhindered love. She wrapped her arms around my neck and cried with me. She stroked my hair and promised it wouldn't always be this hard. She said she didn't know the story God was writing but trusted that He was with us, for us, and near.

I've thought often about that night. Though I don't remember many of the words that were shared, I remember how my heart felt. I remember the deep sadness. But what I remember most is how it felt to have my friend on my lap, her arms entwining my shoulders, my head alongside hers as we wept together. My pain was also hers in a real, deep way. It was one of the most profoundly tender and gentle acts she could have offered on that sad night. She was hope and love in the flesh, manifested in ways I couldn't even articulate needing.

As I think about her with me, it reminds me of how Jesus is with us. Sometimes He is beside us, like she was in that chair alongside mine. But other times He is literally in our lap, engulfing us with love and tenderness.

If you are in a season of despair, loneliness, or grief, take a minute to imagine Jesus sitting on your lap, holding you close. Imagine the weight of Him. Imagine how it would feel to have the Lord wrapping His arms around your shoulders, weeping with you, praying with you, and offering comfort.

You are never, ever alone. He is always with us.

PRAYER

Lord, sit with me in my pain and sadness. Wipe my tears, stroke my hair, and tell me that it won't be like this forever. Share my pain and engulf me with love and tenderness. Thank You for always, always being with me. Amen.

Day 17

some things can't be fixed

I have said these things to you, that in me you may have peace. In the world you will have tribulation. But take heart; I have overcome the world.

John 16:33 ESV

The door slammed hard. The ringing vibrations shook the walls, tilting frames this way and that. I went after my son, pounding my fist on the door he had just whipped shut in my face. My forehead fell effortlessly against it as I jiggled the knob, and tears came—hot and hopeless tears. I turned my body and leaned my back against this barricade blocking me from my teenager. Everything felt impossible.

Some things just can't be fixed. Some relationships can't be forced. Some health issues don't have answers. Some circumstances can't be changed. The temptation in the unfixable places of our lives is to do just that—fix. The temptation is to gather more information, talk to more people, try another method. We are so desperate to make things better. We want peace, solutions, clarity, direction, unity. We want things to go or be a certain way. It is excruciating to live in the tension of what was and what is to come. I hate it. I want things fixed—NOW. I don't like living in the middle. I don't like that I can't make things different than they are.

And here, in the middle of tension, are Jesus's words to us: "Take heart; I have overcome the world." *Take heart.* Could there be more beautiful words? Two words that call my eyes and attention to the heavens, to hope, to the true Fixer. *Take heart.*

My friend, when you are in a situation that is completely defeating, take heart. When you can't make people change, take heart. When you can't fix the problem, take heart. Jesus has overcome the world.

In the most impossible moments, instead of fixing, wait outside the door.

PRAYER

Lord, I'm here. I'm waiting outside the door, fists balled and tears falling. This moment feels absolutely impossible, and I'm waiting for You to show up and fix it all. Except that's not what You said You'd do. You asked me to wait, trust, and hope. You summed it up in two tiny words that together are powerful: take heart. "Take heart, I have overcome . . . and so will you." Thank You, Lord. Help me hang on to the peace those words bring. Amen.

Day 18

plants grow in the dark

Very truly I tell you, unless a kernel of wheat falls to the ground and dies, it remains only a single seed. But if it dies, it produces many seeds.

John 12:24

A long rectangular patch of dirt runs along the side of our house. It's a garden, but no one would call it that at the moment. Pine needles lie like a blanket on top of the soil, an old kale plant stands tall, yellow, and bare, and rusty tools lean on each other in the corner.

It will stay as is for the rest of winter, but when the weather warms up, this patch of dirt will become a garden again—full of lettuce, chard, white radishes, and an abundance of garlic chives.

Though the garden isn't tended well and rain is sporadic, somehow the plants keep growing.

One spring, after an unusual bout of steady rain over several days, the plants were wild with growth, and one of the most surprising things I noticed was how they seemed to grow exponentially at night, without sunlight or any human help.

We're keen to want light in our faith journey. We pray for clarity and direction, and we ask for plans and thoughts on our future. We ask God to grow us, lead us, teach us, mold us, but we're surprised when He does this in the dark, in the middle of the night.

But we can't know light without darkness. We can't know life without death. We can't know morning without night. We can't know growth without first being a seed hidden and planted in the ground.

I'm in that place now. Like a seed, I am soaking in nutrients through mentoring, counseling, and cultivating life-giving relationships. But a seed only becomes a plant through its undoing, its death, and God is breaking me down to build me back up again. He is chiseling the uneven parts of my character so I can better reflect His holiness and goodness. He is revealing the broken parts of my story, the wounds that have stayed open for too long, and His loving hand heals me.

I was afraid to be in the dark, scared of becoming undone, of exposing my hidden darkness to His light. But I'm learning not to fear the dark and instead to embrace this intimate and sacred space with God. He is good in this place, and He is doing good work in me.

PRAYER

Lord, growth can be so painful, and more often than not I wish it didn't have to be. Help me to trust You in the process of dying to myself, healing from past wounds, and becoming more like Jesus. Amen.

Day 19

be gentle with yourself

I have loved you with an everlasting love;
I have drawn you with unfailing kindness.

Jeremiah 31:3

I often feel lost and tired. I struggle with anxiety. And most people would not be able to tell by looking at my life from the outside.

But deep inside, anxiety sounds like a jackhammer pounding against my chest. It feels like waves of nausea making me seasick though I'm lying still on my bed. Anxiety traps me inside an invisible glass jar, where it feels like I'm walking around viewing life through the lens of a camera instead of seeing all the vibrant colors. Though I watch the leaves falling in autumn like gentle rain, I can't truly feel the beauty of the breeze.

I feel numb. Anxiety for me is expressed through insomnia and panic attacks. I grew up cheerful by nature. I love God and serve others, and I have wonderful friends, a loving husband, a passion for God's Word, and a consistent prayer life. But growing up the oldest in a single-parent family, I was much better at being obedient and getting things done, taking care of others, and pushing myself hard rather than taking care of myself and being vulnerable about my needs and desires.

The truth I came to discover is that anxiety doesn't mean our faith is flawed. It doesn't mean we are weak or that we aren't trusting God. These were lies that made me feel ashamed, and God wanted to heal me, not shame me.

The truth is that for those of us who have overcome emotional traumas earlier in our lives because we *have* been strong in faith, God calls us to a deeper journey of healing and an intimate experience of His love.

Jesus wants to gather the pieces of our hearts and the stories that we hide and whisper to us, "What no one wants, I cherish. All the broken moments in your life are beautiful to Me because you were there and so was I. I love you."

When you start to feel anxiety rising in your body and your heart, stop and recognize this moment as an opportunity to let God love you. Don't be hard on yourself. Instead, be gentle with yourself because God's love is gentle. "Your right hand upholds me; and your gentleness makes me great" (Ps. 18:35 NASB).

As I've learned to live as God's beloved, I have been learning to use that phrase—*be gentle with yourself*—as something to rest and breathe into. So take a deep breath and exhale into the loving arms of Jesus, who holds you and says, "It's okay. I've got you. I understand you, and I will take care of you because you are My beloved."

See the gentleness in His eyes for you because He cares about you, your story, your upbringing, and all the anxieties that rise in you. Be kind to yourself and know that you don't have to hide your heart. He sees it all and loves you so very much.

PRAYER

Jesus, I need to hear You say, "It's okay. I've got you. And I understand you. I will take care of you because you are My beloved." I need to see the gentleness in Your eyes and the kindness in Your heart. This is how I heal and thrive and grow. When I feel the familiar rise of anxiety in my body and heart, help me to stop and recognize this as an opportunity to let You love me in Your gentle strength. Amen.

Day 20

your full-circle moment will come

"Therefore, go. I am sending you to Pharaoh so that you may lead my people, the Israelites, out of Egypt."

But Moses asked God, "Who am I that I should go to Pharaoh and that I should bring the Israelites out of Egypt?"

He answered, "I will certainly be with you, and this will be the sign to you that I am the one who sent you: when you bring the people out of Egypt, you will all worship God at this mountain."

Exodus 3:10–12 CSB

The last time I stood on this beach, my faith was exhausted. I had believed for seven years that God would give me a child. I had prayed for a miracle and waited. As I stood in the ocean, I cried out to Him while I let the waves of His constant love wash over me. I was angry and frustrated. I told Him so. I was real with my Savior. I reminded Jesus of His promises and told Him I needed Him to come through.

And He heard me.

I wiped off the salt from my tears and the sand from the beach. That day I boarded a plane with my husband as we headed home from vacation, not sure what the future held. The next month God changed my situation.

61

On August 30, 2012, the pregnancy test was positive. I was carrying my first child. I was overcome with a wave of complete joy. I've never been so amazed, relieved, and thankful.

Fast-forward seven years to August 30, 2019. I stand on that same beach where my tears had mixed with the salt of the Pacific, but now I am playing in the waves with my living, breathing answer to prayer, our miracle daughter, Gabrielle.

When I had planned this trip for my parents, I was thinking about their story, not mine—until I arrived and realized God had brought me full circle. He returned me to the place of fulfilled promise, just like He did for Moses at Mount Sinai. First, there was seven years of waiting, believing God's promises and listening to His voice. Now I had experienced seven years of living in His answer.

I float out on the waves to the sacred spot, but this time with Gabrielle. We talk to Jesus. I thank Him with happy tears for the miracle He gave me in her, for answered prayers, for keeping His promises and bringing me back to remind me of His love for us.

God really comes through on His promises. He will answer your prayers in His timing. He creates new life in all kinds of beautiful ways. God is trying to show you His faithfulness in your life if you will pay attention. Remember what He has done for you, and enjoy His miracles.

PRAYER

Jesus, help me to wait on You for the miracles I am praying for, acknowledge You when You answer, and pay attention to the way You orchestrate my life to show Your sovereignty. Amen.

We have a God
who sits with us in the dark
so we can bear witness to the light.

A God who will never leave or forsake us

and who continues to speak
the language of hope into our sorrow.
When my mind or body or life fails me,
Jesus never will.

—**ALIA JOY**

Day 21

hope

Many, Lord my God,
    are the wonders you have done,
    the things you planned for us.
None can compare with you;
    were I to speak and tell of your deeds,
    they would be too many to declare.

Psalm 40:5

Sometimes mental illness slices through my desire, leaving me gutted and hollow. I don't care if I live or die. I don't care about glory or hope. Indeed, I'd release them all to the darkness.

Sometimes my world feels impossibly small. When my bipolar depression has me in its clutches, sometimes my world's no bigger than the four corners of my pillow holding my head captive for days at a time. Sometimes I'm convinced hope is for those with more money, more talent, more education, more health, more unblemished skin and pearly white teeth.

For the little girl who wore a white pillowcase on her head like a veil and marched past her audience of stuffed animals only to say "I do" to her teddy bear, an empty ring finger in adulthood can feel like a divorce from the life she hoped for, from the dreams she held.

For those who've said goodbyes next to hospital beds and gone home to stare longingly at the side of the bed that will never be slept in again, hope dies.

For those who've peed on a stick month after month, only to realize they've wasted another $14.99 on a test they'll never pass, hope feels cruel.

For those of us who thought our lives would be extraordinary and instead wonder if this is all there is, hope is distracting.

For those of us who struggle to pay our bills, to get up each morning, or to think of another recipe we can make out of the chicken thighs that were on sale, hope seems extravagant.

For those of us who thought we'd do more, be more, have more, see more, know more, but instead face the reality that some prayers aren't answered with "more," we wonder what good hope is.

Is hope a luxury only others can afford?

When hope dies, we often hunker down into reality and say, "This is my portion, this is my cup. This is all I'll ever have, all I'll ever be, all I should ever want."

Sometimes we couch this in snazzy super-spiritual terms like "contentment" and "gratefulness." We might even seem pious and righteous because we have accepted our lot in life and we aren't greedy or selfish, striving or searching.

But we're the servant in the parable who takes his one talent and buries it because he's afraid of his master. He doesn't want to squander what little he has, and goodness knows it's not much, so he risks nothing. When we live like that servant, we've learned not to pray to God as a loving Father. We've learned not to depend on God to preserve us and be our hope.

We don't believe God's intention is for our flourishing. Instead, we embrace scarcity. We believe God's holding out on us, so we resign ourselves to hopelessness and call it faithfulness. We resign ourselves to bitterness and call it prudence.

But Jesus is the hope we have. Not because of what we accomplish or attain, but because when we're disappointed by our lack, our weakness, our loss, we have a God who loves us. Instead of only praying, "I want more!" we can pray, "I want You." The "more" Jesus offers is Himself, our everlasting hope.

We have a God who sits with us in the dark so we can bear witness to the light. A God who will never leave or forsake us and who continues to speak the language of hope into our sorrow. When my mind or body or life fails me, Jesus never will.

PRAYER

Lord, hope seems extravagant, and peace is hard to come by. It feels like too much to even dare ask for hope when sorrow surrounds and pain abounds. And so I will ask that You meet me here, right where I am, just as I am. Speak the language of hope into my sorrow. Help me to want You above wanting more, to remember that You are a loving Father, and to trust that You are my everlasting hope. Amen.

the thing you need to battle distraction and fatigue

In the morning, LORD, you hear my voice;
in the morning I lay my requests before you
and wait expectantly.

Psalm 5:3

I've been feeling it again. That low-grade ache of discontentment. An inner restlessness. Something nagging, gnawing, softly knocking. It's an unnamed longing for something more—even on the good days when I finally catch my breath, catch up on laundry, or make it to bedtime without being called a "mean, mean mommy."

I don't know why it takes me so long to recognize the source—God's still, small voice calling again.

I've been choosing the allure of glowing screens and too many late-night scrolling minutes. I yearn for quiet solitude, yet I tether myself to the noise of hundreds of "friends" I don't know beyond likes and comments.

The evidence of my digital vegging indulgence shows up the next morning in dark under-eye circles and two more snooze cycles. I'm too tired and distracted to hear God call, *Come to Me. Connect with Me.*

It's not like I never read my Bible. It's not like I don't pray. I'm good with God, right? But what if doing enough to spiritually get by isn't the point? We need to listen to our longings and admit when there's something out of whack with our lived-out priorities.

My soul hungers for *more*. But more social media, viral videos, and mindless TV aren't going to cut it.

We were cut out for divine connection.

Created for intimacy.

Hand-picked for relationship.

Wired for worship.

We've got a God-sized gap nothing else can fill. Let's recognize the ways we've been trying to fill it—and stop. Let's say no to what pulls us away from the Gap-Filler and instead press into Him. But how?

There's no one-size-fits-all formula, no right or wrong way to spend time with Jesus. For me, I've found nothing better than starting my day with Scripture open, pen to paper, listening.

God's never not shown up to meet me.

The struggles of our lives, the crises, and the daily grind are real. Urgent things demand immediate doing. Desirous things draw us to their company. Attention-grabbing things that feel in-the-moment important but lack eternal significance. They all vie hard for our focus. But we don't have to live consumed by noise that is not His voice.

In the morning I reach for my alarm and remind myself that I'm not getting up for Facebook or Instagram or email. I pull the chain on my stained-glass desk lamp, flooding the darkness with light, and remind myself I'm not rising early to check more off my list.

I rise for Him.

PRAYER

Lord, may Your voice be one I cannot ignore, no matter how still or small. Give me strength to avoid the pull

of digital vegging and instead turn to You. Remind me
that I am not made to seek Facebook or Instagram; I am
made to seek You. Today may this truth be reflected by
my screen time (or lack thereof). Amen.

Day 23

embracing your season

Blessed is the one . . .
　　whose delight is in the law of the LORD,
　　and who meditates on his law day and night.
That person is like a tree planted by streams of water,
　　which yields its fruit in season
and whose leaf does not wither—
　　whatever they do prospers.

Psalm 1:1–3

Life begins and ends, and in the middle is the dash you find on a tombstone. The middle is made up of hills and valleys, victories and losses, seasons of dreaming and seasons of accomplishing.

And that's where I often find myself—smack dab in the middle.

There are dreams and visions I have for my life that have yet to be achieved. I'm at a day job I don't want to be at forever. I want to get married one day. I would like to have more resources to bless others with. And all of it is okay. Now is not forever.

I used to feel guilty about wanting more out of my life. I thought to want more was to be ungrateful for what I had or for the season I was in, but I realize now that I can want more and be grateful for today at the same time.

In Psalm 1, the psalmist says that the blessed person delights in God's Word day in and day out. They meditate on it, and that allows them to be rooted in Him and yield forth fruit in season.

Planting and harvesting is a process that only happens over time. When Jesus is what we seek, we will find Him in every season.

The best part about seasons is that they don't last. If you're patient and fully present in the season you're in, there's a new one right around the corner. And God is always doing a new thing.

So I've learned that being in the middle is okay. God is here with me and you, ready to fill us with peace in the now and hope for the not yet. He will lead us through it.

PRAYER

Lord, help me hang on during this middle season. Help me to seek Your face during this time when I long for more yet don't want to go back to what was. Give me patience to be fully present right where I am and to see the new things You are doing. Amen.

Day 24

the worthy cost of being an ally

Greater love has no one than this: to lay down one's life for one's friends.

John 15:13

My body felt like it was on fire. Like a nerve exposed, every limb and finger burned with a raw and visceral pain as I helplessly stood at a vendor's table and was refused service. I'll never forget the way the hairs on my neck stood up and my breath caught in my throat. The man wouldn't even look at me. As soon as he saw me coming, he turned around, and even now as I spoke to him, all I could see was his back.

What started as an everyday shopping trip had turned into a nightmare. I had spent the same twenty minutes in line as everyone else to receive a free promotional bag. But now, as I tried saying "Excuse me" and other things to get the man's attention, it slowly became clear that this backward stance was his way of saying I wasn't worthy, that my brown skin disqualified me from the same opportunity as the other women in the store. I was being rejected simply because of who I was.

I felt alone and helpless. I didn't know if I should stand my ground and demand the bag or just grab my things and leave. Could this man really be so cruel? I tried one more desperate attempt to be treated like a human being, but I could hear my voice begin to shake, and now I just wanted to find a hole to crawl into and hide.

But right before I fled, I heard another voice beside me say, "Sir, give her a bag." I turned in shock to see a woman who had been behind me in line now standing next to me. Her eyes had power and her face was unquestioningly stern. Only then did the man turn back around. He never looked me in the eyes, but he seemed to be captivated by hers.

She then continued, "This woman deserves a bag. Same as the rest of us. Give her one now, please."

I couldn't believe it at first. A person I had never met before was speaking up for me. This stranger was choosing to be my ally. Though we didn't know each other, she believed that speaking up on my behalf was the right thing to do, no matter the cost. The vendor could be cruel to her, too, but she didn't care. She was willing to lay down her own rights to defend mine.

In John 15, Jesus commands us to love one another, and in verse 13 He explains that the greatest form of love is to lay down our life for a friend's. As believers, we are to put the interests of others above our own. This is what Jesus did for us. Though we were still sinners, Christ died for us, giving up His own life so that we could be saved. Now we too must show others love in the same way that Jesus loved us.

Perhaps you're that woman at the back of the line, seeing injustice unfold in front of you, but your feet feel nailed to the ground. Perhaps you feel that desire to help but don't know what to say, and the words just won't come. You worry that you'll look silly or be criticized. To you I say, "Take heart. Keep trying. Even the little things go a long way." We can physically stand by someone, even if all we do is stutter. We don't have to have a long speech. Sometimes just saying, "This isn't right," is enough to let the world know you won't passively accept what's happening. And if criticism comes, let it come. Jesus took much worse for us.

This is the worthy cost of being an ally. That day in the store, a complete stranger modeled the love of Christ to me. She was willing to be my ally no matter the repercussions, and I will always be grateful for her courage.

PRAYER

Jesus, You showed the ultimate way to lay down one's life for one's friends. Give me courage to keep trying, even in the little things, to be an ally for others. Help me to let the potential for criticism not get in the way of doing what is right and good. Thank You for showing me just what that looks like and for taking much worse for me. Amen.

forgiveness is a gift we give ourselves when we offer it to others

Be kind and compassionate to one another, forgiving each other, just as in Christ God forgave you.

Ephesians 4:32

I was standing at the mailbox and opening an invitation when a flood of insecurity and resentment washed over me.

A decade earlier, and just two weeks before I was moving away, a good friend got fed up with me and let me know it in front of some other friends. In the middle of a battle with depression, I didn't have the capacity to process her criticism or work through the conflict at that time, so our friendship ended.

Ten years passed, and by God's grace (plus years of counseling and medication) I was set free from the pain of my past. Or so I thought.

Holding the invitation to an event where I'd likely see that person, I realized I had not forgiven her. I could try to ignore the invite and the pain, or I could pursue the freedom of forgiveness.

Two weeks later, my stomach rumbled with nausea as I filled in the blank on my RSVP with a courageous *yes*.

I read and prayed through Scriptures and listened to sermons about forgiving others. I journaled memories of what happened and asked God to show me His perspective—and even hers.

During the three-hour drive to the event, I had worship music and teaching on God's forgiveness on repeat. *Lord, drench me with the healing power of Your forgiveness and love for me so I don't walk in feeling like the broken girl who moved away ten years ago,* I prayed. I wanted a confidence that could not be shaken, no matter what happened.

When I got there, the most unexpected feeling came over me: I *wanted* to find the friend who'd hurt me and apologize for whatever I had done to upset her. It didn't take long before we saw each other. She smiled and stood up to hug me. Later we talked about what had happened and apologized for hurting each other.

Forgiveness is a gift we give ourselves when we offer it to others. In doing so, we don't forgive so we can forget. We forgive so we can be set free.

PRAYER

Lord, drench me with the healing power of Your forgiveness and love for me so that I can truly forgive. I want to be set free. Help me forgive so that I may indeed be set free from the hold of anger and hurt, and experience the healing that comes with such freedom. Thank You, Jesus, for showing us what it looks like to be kind and compassionate to one another, forgiving each other, just as in Christ God forgave us. Amen.

Day 26

on fear and sending our kids to school

"But I will be with you," the Lord said to him.

Judges 6:16 CSB

I have a second grader, a kindergartner, and a preschooler. I'm not sure how that happened (weren't they just little babies?!), and I'm not entirely sure how I feel about school.

If I'm honest, my biggest emotion is fear, because schools are no longer always safe places. The news of shootings in public places haunts my heart. Movie theaters. Malls. Churches. Concerts. Elementary school classrooms.

Classrooms.

I fear that when I say goodbye to my children in the morning, they won't come home in the afternoon.

I know that death could come for any of us on any day and at any time, but there's something soul-level jarring about the suddenness of death and the shock of terror when it happens in what should be a safe space.

And classrooms should be safe places.

Some of my emotion is fueled by my own anxious tendencies. Some of it is fueled by actual happenings in the world.

All of it is fueled by fear.

Fear displaces almost every other emotion. It kicks out joy, and it steamrolls peace. It takes up the space where trust should reside. Fear leaves a bitter taste in what could otherwise be sweet situations and circumstances. Fear swallows me when I give it space. I think I'm giving fear an inch, and it unfolds into a mile.

The only way I can even begin to combat fear is to focus in sharply on God and God's response to others who have trusted Him in spite of their fear.

Gideon was one such fearful person. Throughout his story in Judges 6, we can see God's patience and care for His fearful servant. God calls Gideon to deliver Israel from the grasp of the Midianites, and right away Gideon asks God a bunch of scared questions. He asks God for proof. He asks God to choose someone else. In his fear, he panics. Then he focuses in and gets the job done.

And the whole time, the Lord reassures him. God tells Gideon that he is a warrior. God tells Gideon that He will be with him. God tells him that he will succeed. God doesn't rush Gideon through his fear; rather, God stands with him and gives Gideon what he needs to overcome it.

There are dozens of stories throughout the Bible about fellow fear-overcomers: Jonah, Sarah, Abraham, Esther, Daniel, Moses—people afraid of what or where they were called to be.

Friends, we are surrounded by a cloud of witnesses who have trusted in the One who crushes fear. It bolsters my courage to bring their stories to mind and to tuck into my heart God's response of patience and love. God didn't make them feel silly about their fear, but instead offered strength and peace, placing His great hand on their backs and gently pushing them forward.

Which is just what I need.

For me, taking heart looks like believing in and leaning on the God who demolishes fear. It looks like sending my kids to school. It looks like believing with all my strength that God stands with my kids. It looks like remembering that God goes first, especially into the places where I cannot. He goes before.

God is there, ready and waiting for our kids.

They do not walk through any doors alone.

The only One who can accompany our kids and provide everything they need is standing by them already. We hold their hands, and God holds them close.

PRAYER

Lord, I can't protect my children from everything, and that terrifies me sometimes. When I am afraid for my children, help me to trust in You. You love them and know them. You care for them more than I ever could. Be my strength, my anchor, and my peace. Amen.

Day 27

unseen disability

Finally, all of you should be of one mind. Sympathize with each other. Love each other as brothers and sisters. Be tenderhearted, and keep a humble attitude.

1 Peter 3:8 NLT

People have always said my husband looks too young to be retired, and after many years he's grown used to the questions and questioning looks. He had hoped for a long career in the army, but God had other plans, and my husband retired in his mid-twenties.

But what people aren't seeing as they talk to a seemingly healthy young man is the scar partially hidden by his hairline. If they looked closely, they would see a long scar from the top of his head down around the front of his ear. And if they really paid attention, they would see the indent in his skull where plates and screws now reside.

These are the telltale signs of a craniotomy. My husband had a giant brain aneurysm that had to be fixed in extreme ways—ways that have changed his life and mine from that day forward. He is one of the many people in this world living with an unseen disability, an invisible illness.

He doesn't need a wheelchair. He isn't missing an arm or leg. He looks pretty normal to anyone passing by. For people to really know, he would need to wear a big sign that says,

"I have had a brain aneurysm and brain surgery, resulting in brain injury."

What people don't see is his daily pain. People can't see that he might not always find his words quickly. People don't know he lost his speech for a time and had to learn to find words again. People can't see he's forgetful. They don't know he takes all sorts of medications and visits doctors often. They don't know that his brain doesn't quite work the same way it once did.

He has needs that aren't visible, and so many other people do as well. You would never guess that many people you have been in contact with who look just fine and normal on the outside are really hurting, sick, or suffering.

We never know what hardship someone is walking through. We don't know what it takes for some people to keep going day by day.

We don't wear signs spelling out how heartbroken we are, how much pain we are in, how worried we are. Imagine the pain we would know if we each walked around wearing a sign that says we have a chronic illness, we lost our job, we have a sick child, we buried a parent, or our spouse left.

This difficult journey with my husband has taught me a great lesson. Looks are deceiving. On the outside, people certainly can look like they have it all together, but that doesn't mean they do. Everyone has something they are struggling with or pain no one can see. Never be so quick to judge what you think you see, what you think you know.

Ultimately, God knows what each person is going through, and He wants us to be His hands and feet and extend compassion to them. May we be gentler and more patient with one another, and may God open our hearts and minds to see others through His eyes.

Lord, help people to see the invisible pain in me, and help me to see it in them. Open my heart and mind to see others through Your eyes with gentleness, compassion, and kindness. May I care for others with the same grace You've given me. Amen.

God brings beauty from our brokenness

when we share our stories
and bear one another's burdens.
Sometimes it's awkward and uncomfortable.
Sometimes it's messy.
But God meets us there.

—DORINA LAZO GILMORE

Day 28

recovering from racism

> But you are a chosen people, a royal priesthood, a holy nation, God's special possession, that you may declare the praises of him who called you out of darkness into his wonderful light. Once you were not a people, but now you are the people of God; once you had not received mercy, but now you have received mercy.
>
> 1 Peter 2:9–10

The first time I was called the N-word—by a little white girl who was barely five years old—I faced a remarkable choice. Listen to hate? Or listen to God?

But who does God say that I am?

I'd heard that question my entire life, especially as a follower of Christ, but I heard it in a new way in recent years as the burden of racial hatred seemed to worsen. I looked wrongly for a remedy though—not from God or even myself, but from people who caused pain.

So, that five-year-old girl? *Wherever she may be*, she's *the one at fault*, I argued. *And me? Why should I be responsible for healing my own heartache? Ridiculous*, I thought. *Not my job, not my problem.*

Except it was my problem. When we hang on to old wounds, the people who hurt us aren't dragged down, *we* are. Thus, after decades of slogging through old racial wounds, I finally sought God and prayed, *Who do You say that I am?*

Sure, I'd heard others' put-downs. One teacher in my junior high school called me "nobody" for an entire school year, never once calling on me when I raised my hand to answer her questions in class.

Or when my family set out to buy our first home in Denver, what did my parents face? Race-based covenants ("Only whites allowed") and warnings: "Great danger ahead! Did you know there are negroes trying to move here? Let's get together and protect ourselves!"

Really? Me? A great danger?

But what does *God* say?

For years, I forgot what God says about me, until I finally heard God's declarations of how He sees me—and also sees you. Dare we accept His healing words? If so, say them out loud with me:

I am God's own—valuable and priceless!

Yes, God Himself created us in His own image—"male and female he created," says Genesis 1:27. Thus, we're His beautiful image-bearers—or in Latin, his *Imago Dei*. We're no shabby, secondhand, worthless imitations. Instead, we matter to God.

I am loved—first by God!

Other people don't know this, says 1 John 3:1, because "they don't know him." Good and right truth, but it gets better.

I am chosen by God—royal too!

Unlike the days of Hosea, when the Lord God said, "I will no longer show love to the people of Israel or forgive them" (Hos. 1:6 NLT), look how things have changed! Peter says that now we are a "chosen people"—yes, "royal priests" (1 Pet. 2:9 NLT).

Even better?

I am victorious! My future is bright!

"You are the light of the world" (Matt. 5:14). And we are victorious (1 Cor. 15:57), more than conquerors (Rom. 8:37), and citizens of heaven (Phil. 3:20) with a glorious future (Rom. 8:18).

So, when people don't see me or you for who we are, that is their problem—because they don't know God. Until they do, we must know Him for ourselves—hearing Him sing over us, calling us by His own name. His people. His creation. His beloved. His own.

And knowing that? We know it all.

PRAYER

Thank You, Lord, for giving me the exact words that describe who I truly am. I am Your own, valuable and priceless! I am loved, chosen, and victorious! When I doubt or when I am doubted, remind me, Lord, that I matter to You. I am Your beloved, called by Your own name. Thank You. Amen.

Day 29

new life for dry bones

> GOD, the Master, told the dry bones, "Watch this: I'm bringing
> the breath of life to you and you'll come to life."
>
> Ezekiel 37:5 MSG

It's a mad dash between trying to get the rebellious four-year-old to nap and dabbing on enough under-eye concealer to look presentable while finishing the imminently due assignment before running out the door. The crowded campus parking lot with narrow spots is easy to navigate compared to the skill it takes to delegate three kids' schedules and pull away from the fray.

Huffing slightly, I climb the final flight of stairs and make it to my seat with but a breath of time to spare. We do introductions, then go over the course syllabus for English 510: Literature and the Bible. "Now, let's dive into our first activity," the professor says. "Turn with me to Ezekiel chapter 37."

He reads from *The Message* version a story about dry bones. "God grabbed me. God's Spirit took me up and set me down in the middle of an open plain strewn with bones."

I follow along on my Bible app, taking in the story to the cadence of the professor's voice.

He stammers a bit, but my eyes stay locked on the words. "So I prophesied, just as he commanded me. Then breath entered them and they came alive!"

87

I glance up and understand the cause of the professor's pause. He's choked up, trying hard to swallow the lump in his throat and not let the welling tears spill over.

He regains his composure and finishes the passage. "I'll breathe my life into you and you'll live. Then I'll lead you straight back to your land and you'll realize that I am God. I've said it and I'll do it."

The white-haired professor's eyes are rimmed a bit red. He cracks a smile and gently shakes his head. He's been teaching for thirty-seven years and didn't expect to get emotional, he explains. Then, instead of launching into an explanation of the literary devices used in the text or discussing how this passage mirrors another piece of literature, the man behind the podium looks out into the eyes of each attentive graduate student and says this:

"As we study the Bible this semester, it's not just academic— it's the Word of God. You can study the Bible, as many have, and not believe it. But I *believe* it. As Christians, the Holy Spirit speaks through the Word."

Now the instructor isn't the only one visibly moved.

We could spend three hours every Wednesday afternoon dissecting Scripture and analyzing literature, and that would be fine. But my dear professor understands that the Bible isn't just another book. It's the living Word, breathed into Spirit-inspired life by the same God who resurrected dry bones and who wants to do life-breathing work in us too.

And it makes me think, what other areas in our lives could we get by with "fine" yet miss out on the fullness of God's Word and the possibility of experiencing new life?

What if we believed God could breathe life into the weariness of marriage or motherhood? Meet us with living hope in the middle of the witching hour, homework meltdowns, and bedtime battles?

What if God doesn't want us just to pin a verse on the bulletin board at work, but He wants us to pin the Word to our hearts and believe it and be changed by it?

What if we didn't shuffle through our church Bible study or morning quiet time out of obligation to check off a spiritual to-do box? What if we asked God to use His Word to choke us up with the beauty and power of truth so that we might see new life spring forth from the most barren, unlikely places?

I think we've all got some dry bones in our personal valley. Let's ask God to breathe new life into them and then watch in believing expectation.

PRAYER

God, my life—my soul—feels dry. I can't quite put my finger on why, or maybe it's that everything is getting to me, but I am worn and weary. Your Word is life, so I'm turning to You and Your Word today. Meet me, God. Breathe new life into me. Amen.

Day 30

he will meet you
in your mourning

She turned to leave and saw someone standing there. It was Jesus, but she didn't recognize him. "Dear woman, why are you crying?" Jesus asked her. "Who are you looking for?"

She thought he was the gardener. "Sir," she said, "if you have taken him away, tell me where you have put him, and I will go and get him."

"Mary!" Jesus said.

She turned to him and cried out, "Rabboni!" (which is Hebrew for "Teacher").

John 20:14–16 NLT

While I was waiting in line at the coffee shop on the other side of town, a familiar voice called my name. Before I turned around, I knew the face that would greet me. We weren't meeting there to catch up. In fact, I had no idea my friend would arrive moments after I walked through the door.

But I've heard him say my name so often that I know his tone and cadence well enough to determine his identity with my eyes closed or my back turned.

The same is true for my family and close friends. We've known each other so long that if they yelled my name in a crowded room or left a voicemail from an unknown number and simply spoke the two syllables that make up my first name, I would immediately know who was calling for me.

I've heard my name on their lips dozens, if not hundreds, of times.

Perhaps that's why John 20 never fails to bring tears to my eyes.

The chapter begins in darkness. Mary Magdalene discovers the empty tomb, the miracle of resurrection, before the sun begins to rise. She is the first to witness the greatest promise kept, but in her confusion and grief, she runs to the disciples, fearfully and perhaps frantically saying, "They have taken the Lord's body out of the tomb, and we don't know where they have put him!"

After Peter and John run to the tomb to confirm Mary's account, Scripture tells us they go home.

But Mary stays.

As she weeps, she stoops down to look inside and sees two angels in the place where she last saw her Lord and Friend. "Dear woman, why are you crying?" the angels ask her.

I like to imagine that I would've understood the miracle before my eyes, but I believe that Mary couldn't see past the tears clouding her own. Swallowed by grief and doubt, it's likely that she didn't realize she was in the presence of angels. After all, she replies, "Because they have taken away my Lord and I don't know where they have put him," before turning to leave.

And then dear Mary literally runs into her Lord.

She doesn't recognize the very One she is looking for, but He meets her exactly where she is and calls her by name.

"Dear woman, why are you crying?" Jesus asks. "Who are you looking for?"

Thinking him to be the gardener, she replies, "Sir, if you have taken him away, tell me where you have put him, and I will go and get him."

And then with one word, her entire world changes. Jesus speaks her name, and tears fill my eyes two thousand years later because in that moment she knows.

She knows His tone and His cadence. She knows exactly what her name sounds like when spoken on His lips. She had remained cloaked in darkness and doubt with "dear woman," unable to see past her circumstances, but at the sound of her name light breaks through.

The same is still true for us today. You are free to show up exactly as you are. Come with your grief, your doubt, your confusion, and your fears. Jesus won't run away; He won't disappear. Instead, He comes close. He meets us in our mourning and sees us in our sadness. His tone is gentle and kind, patient and loving. Do you hear it? He's calling your name.

PRAYER

Jesus, I long to hear You, to recognize Your voice saying my name. Break through with Your light. Come close with Your gentleness. Call my name and change my world with one word, Lord. I want to bring my grief, doubt, confusion, and fears to You in confidence. Amen.

Day 31

a faith that laughs

She is clothed with strength and dignity;
she can laugh at the days to come.

Proverbs 31:25

I knew something was amiss the moment she came down the stairs.

Hmm. Something's different.

Her hair was the same and her outfit was familiar. But my twelve-year-old definitely looked odd. I couldn't quite put my finger on it until . . .

Good heavens, her eyebrows. She no longer has eyebrows!

Yes, my dark-haired girl somehow managed to rid herself of her eyebrow hair. And the result was—how shall I say?—hilarious.

"Um, what happened to your eyebrows, darling?"

It was all I could do not to bust out laughing. I'm pretty sure Jesus can be credited for my restraint. Left to my own devices, I would've been doubled over gasping for air. Alas, the Holy Spirit intervened.

"I cut them off," she said matter-of-factly.

"Why'd you do that?" I was dying to know.

"Because one was too hairy." She paused, glanced at the floor. "But then I needed to do the other one too."

93

Bless her, my girl is nothing if not excessive. My greatest challenge in parenting her into adulthood is teaching her self-control, patience, and restraint.

Ugh. Sounds familiar.

Truth is, we both needed to laugh. So we walked through her decision-making process and the repercussions, and then had a good old-fashioned laugh. It was good medicine for both of us.

Parenting hasn't been an easy road for me. With six kids and two adults, all of whom have experienced varying degrees of loss and trauma, it seems like I spend most of my parenting time putting out fires. I see the sweet-and-easy social media posts of mamas with their adorable and well-behaved children—children with eyebrows intact—and I ache for an easier story, a more comfortable and conflict-free parenting road.

But I'm learning the gift of laughter. It's okay to cry some days, to scream into my pillow on others. But I want to be the kind of woman who knows how to dig deep to find hilarity in the hard. "She is clothed with strength and dignity," Proverbs 31:25 says. "She can laugh at the days to come."

Laughter, too, is a grace. It's evidence of God's ability to soften my heart. Because when I can learn to find joy in the worst of circumstances, that means I trust Him to handle it all. It's a faith that laughs in spite of the many reasons not to.

Even with missing eyebrows.

PRAYER

Laughter. God, sweet laughter! Give me a chance to laugh today. The kind of deep belly laugh that springs from pure joy, found even in the worst of circumstances. If I can laugh, I just might make it through. Give me a faith that laughs, Lord. Amen.

in the waiting

While he was with them, he commanded them not to leave Jerusalem, but to wait for the Father's promise.

Acts 1:4 CSB

Young, bright-eyed, and eager to mark a generation of women for Jesus, I scribbled down my to-do list as quickly as the conference presenters poured out their advice on how to take our ministry to the next level. I admired these leaders. They were accomplished and well-spoken, and their list of accolades announced that they were not only women to learn from but also to follow. Yes, I wanted to do what they were doing. How exciting to be used by God in such a tangible way.

I raced home after their charge, and in between the babies' nap times and laundry piles, work deadlines and bill paying, I started dreaming a God-sized vision.

And then I prayed. And waited. I knew something exciting was coming my way. I petitioned. And waited some more. "Don't forget, I'm your girl, Lord."

Crickets.

So I pleaded. "Lord, I'm eager and ready to make Your name known. Reveal Your calling for my life. Use me."

And then it was as if I heard Him whisper, "Jen, wait. Your list is good, but stay rooted in your present Jerusalem, your home, and My plan will be greater."

I thought maybe I'd heard Him wrong. Stay put and wait?

I wonder if the disciples felt that same way after Christ's resurrection. Not only had they seen Jesus perform miraculous signs and wonders but they'd witnessed their risen Lord go from death to life. Can you even imagine? They touched His nail-pierced hands. He was alive! If I were the disciples, I'd round up doubters from every possible place and sprint to showcase Christ's great works. Yet Jesus's response in Acts 1:4 stuns me.

He commands the disciples to stay put, to wait. I can only imagine the questions they tossed Jesus's way after that declaration.

"But why wait, Lord?" I'm sure they felt a sense of urgency to go, yet they were commanded not to leave Jerusalem but to wait. I know Jesus wasn't telling the disciples to sit and do nothing, so I pondered new perspectives and priorities.

In our culture that screams bigger, better, smarter, stronger, faster, and famous, it's challenging to quiet our hearts to see smaller as significant and slower as sanctified. In a world of quick fixes and googling instantaneous answers, waiting isn't weakness or unwillingness. Waiting requires strength and resolve.

I tucked away that conference to-do list for nearly twenty years. It was a good list with a God-honoring vision, but His calling for that season encouraged me to stay put for decades. It was there that He carved true contentment: a new legacy. My God-sized dream looked like showing up for small moments, working faithfully in jobs I didn't love, opening doors to neighbors who needed a safe place to share, and making one more meal when I had just finished cleaning up the last. It looked like waiting through seasons of sickness and unemployment, through broken relationships and eventual restoration.

Staying put revealed God's Word fleshed out in everyday, seemingly insignificant moments, and I can honestly say that nothing beats the life-giving abundance that comes from choosing to be deeply rooted and invested right where He has us—in our Jerusalem, our workplace, our school, our everyday table.

I'm still waiting for the place the Lord prepares in advance for me and my family, wherever that may be. But aren't we all?

Each day I wake up expectant, because it's in the waiting that all God's promises are fulfilled.

PRAYER

Lord, I'm weary of waiting. All I hear is crickets when I expect angel choruses. I'd even settle for a still, small voice whispering in the wind. But if this is where You want me, this is where I will stay, and I will wait for You right here in my Jerusalem. May I have strength and patience in this season of seemingly insignificant moments, knowing that each one is a building block to a firmer foundation. Amen.

Day 33

flourishing in community

But blessed is the one who trusts in the Lord,
  whose confidence is in him.
They will be like a tree planted by the water
  that sends out its roots by the stream.
It does not fear when heat comes;
  its leaves are always green.
It has no worries in a year of drought
  and never fails to bear fruit.

Jeremiah 17:7–8

She hung back in the sanctuary until most of the women cleared out from the event. She waved me over and asked if we could talk.

"I'm looking for someone to mentor me," she said with dark eyes shining. "I know you are really busy, but would you consider it?"

I had just finished emceeing a two-day women's gathering with the theme of discipleship. I paused at first because I didn't feel "old enough" to be her mentor. What wisdom did I have to offer? The more we chatted, the more I realized she really wanted someone to run alongside her in this race called life. She was a mother, a leader, a woman of color who was longing for accountability and deeper friendship.

That courageous question changed the course of both our lives. Although Yazmin and I are from different cultures and have different upbringings, different personalities, and different ministries, God brought us together to sharpen each other. Our differences are our strength. We've done some deep heart work together—sharing vulnerably, confessing our sins, praying together, and encouraging each other, especially on the hardest part of the trail.

We have learned the power of presence. Although I am ten years older, we journey together shoulder-to-shoulder. We don't waste time comparing ourselves to each other. We think of ways to collaborate and spur each other on to good choices. Our friendship is marked by mutual edification.

The prophet Jeremiah talks about how those who trust in the Lord are like trees planted together near the water. He paints a picture of these trees with leaves that stay green. They do not fear when the heat comes. They are not anxious when the water is low. They have confidence in God's provision. They continue to produce fruit.

Friend, we are designed to flourish in community. God brings beauty from our brokenness when we share our stories and bear one another's burdens. Sometimes it's awkward and uncomfortable. Sometimes it's messy. But God meets us there. He does not want us to run through this life in isolation, where the enemy can speak lies and distract us. God wants all of us to experience His abundance by flourishing together.

Yazmin and I set our eyes on the finish line together. Finishing well and leading our people to God's glory is the goal. Some days we run; other days we kneel.

PRAYER

Lord, I want to experience Your abundance within my own community. My heart is open, and so are my hands. Lead me to a place with people who are ready to run together, knowing that Your glory is the goal. Amen.

Day 34

what we need to remember at midlife (and always)

Blessed be the God and Father of our Lord Jesus Christ, who has blessed us in Christ with every spiritual blessing in the heavenly places, even as he chose us in him before the foundation of the world, that we should be holy and blameless before him. In love he predestined us for adoption to himself as sons through Jesus Christ, according to the purpose of his will, to the praise of his glorious grace, with which he has blessed us in the Beloved. In him we have redemption through his blood, the forgiveness of our trespasses, according to the riches of his grace, which he lavished upon us, in all wisdom and insight making known to us the mystery of his will, according to his purpose, which he set forth in Christ.

Ephesians 1:3–9 ESV

I awakened on New Year's Day grinning like a Cheshire cat, expectant for what the new year offered: possibilities. But then, like a bully, my next thought sucker-punched me: *In three months I'll turn fifty.*

My heart sank as darkness extinguished my joy, shortcomings and lack clobbering me. *Shouldn't I have achieved more by now? Why haven't I accomplished my goals? What is God's purpose for my life?*

Pulling the covers over my head, a silent scream erupted: *I NEED TO BE INSPIRED!*

Milestone birthdays demand a lot of attention, don't they? They evoke an emotional response that in-between birthdays don't seem to produce, especially the older we get.

Those round numbers feel like they're marking something important, an extraordinary dispensation of time. While twenty, thirty, and forty are biggies, fifty is a doozy. (I can only imagine future milestones.)

No matter your exact age, midlife is complicated. The issues that surface have bigger implications with far-reaching repercussions. It's a juggling act of circus proportions, involving so many things at once—aging parents, challenging children, career setbacks, financial pressures, health concerns, shifting friendships, marriage stresses, general void.

Meanwhile, inside your heart and mind inner turmoil swirls. It's tempting to compare the entirety of your life to the soundbites and highlights of others, a selective exercise that by design will always leave you lacking. Comparison makes room for feelings of worthlessness, insignificance, and inadequacy to slither in.

Midlife can be disorienting. Like a milestone birthday, it demands attention. And when your focus is diverted from God to your circumstances, it's easy to wander off course.

That's where I found myself the morning of my fiftieth year—desperate and disoriented, forgetting who God tells me I am regardless of my age or season in life. His Word tells me I am created in His image to be His image-bearer to the world, the seed of incredible purpose! Ephesians 1 paints a beautiful portrait of how we're equipped to carry this out: blessed with *every* spiritual blessing, chosen, loved, holy and blameless before God through Christ. We're adopted as children, lavished with grace, redeemed, forgiven, and much more.

Inspiration is always near when we maintain focus on God and take Him at His word. We are beloved daughters of the King of kings, worthy, significant, and more than adequate because of Jesus in us.

No matter our age or season.

PRAYER

God, I come to You desperate and disoriented, ready for a reminder to bowl me over. Your Word tells me who I truly am: blessed with every spiritual blessing, chosen, loved, holy and blameless before God through Christ, adopted as Your child, lavished with grace, redeemed, forgiven, and much more. Help me remember these truths when the lies swirl and sound more convincing than Your actualities. May I maintain focus on You and Your Word, no matter what. Amen.

when you're tired of praying about that difficult relationship

And he told them . . . that they ought always to pray and not lose heart.

Luke 18:1 ESV

After another maddening conversation, I take a sharp turn into the bathroom. I shut the door and lean on the pedestal sink as I look at myself in the mirror. Weary words swirl like smoke around me: *Why must this relationship be so difficult? And really, why do I keep bothering with it anyway?*

I close my eyes and open them again, frustration carrying me to the conclusion that things will never change. We're at a dead-end country lane, and all we can do is back up and travel the same gravel over and over.

It's too far-gone, too hope-gone.

My attitude resembles that of a man from the household of Jairus as told in the book of Luke. Jairus, a synagogue ruler, pleads with Jesus to come to his house because his only daughter is dying. While Jesus and Jairus are still en route, a man from Jairus's house meets them and tells Jairus, "Your daughter is dead. . . . Don't bother the teacher anymore" (Luke 8:49).

Jairus's daughter died.

With circumstances too far-gone, why bother Jesus?

My own disappointment asks the same thing. This relationship is too hopeless, too dead. Why bother Jesus with this anyway? So I give up on my prayers, on Him. I'm just tired of hoping, tired of the letdown.

And then I'm smacked upside the head with a startling reality: in cherry-picked difficulties like this relationship, I act like an unbeliever.

I know Christ can do all things. And indeed, He proves it with Jairus's daughter. "Hearing this, Jesus said to Jairus, 'Don't be afraid; just believe, and she will be healed.' . . . He took her by the hand and said, 'My child, get up!' Her spirit returned, and at once she stood up" (Luke 8:50, 54–55).

With one touch, Jesus raises the dead. With one sentence, He breathes new life into relationships.

So I don't give up on prayer, but I give my prayers up to the throne of God. We can't always talk to people about God, but we can always talk to God about people. Nothing is too far-gone for Jesus to move. We may not see healing at work on this earth, but we trust the Healer at work.

No, my broken relationship doesn't look different, but my heart does—if only a little. It sees a new picture, one changing from hope-gone to hope-dawn.

PRAYER

With one touch, Jesus, You raise the dead. With one sentence, You breathe new life into relationships. You still do miracles today, and You're still doing miracles in my life. Nothing is too far-gone for You to move; I know You can do all things, as You did with Jairus's daughter. Bring my heart back to life, Lord. Move me toward You. Amen.

laying down my privilege and holding space for others

> Instead he emptied himself
> by assuming the form of a servant,
> taking on the likeness of humanity.
> And when he had come as a man,
> he humbled himself by becoming obedient
> to the point of death—
> even to death on a cross.
>
> Philippians 2:7–8 CSB

I read about children separated from their parents at the US-Mexico border, detained in facilities that aren't fit for human beings, trauma forever being etched into their lives. I read about the anniversary of the death of another black man killed, with no justice in sight. I pound my chest at the racism and fear-driven rhetoric that has threatened the lives of immigrants, of refugees, of people of color. Friends have lost their husbands to tragic deaths, marriages are falling apart even as they've just begun, and it all seems too much to hold, too much to take in at the same time. Death and grief and injustice and sadness crash relentlessly around me, and there isn't enough room to take a breath.

And if I'm honest with myself, half of me wants to look away, to hide from the pain of those around me. I want to shut my

105

eyes, put my hands over my ears, and pretend that I don't have the power to change anything, that I'm not responsible to carry the burdens of others.

But it's a privilege to be on the outer ripples of pain, to even have the *choice* to look away. It's a privilege not to be inconvenienced by the lives of others with the ease of clicking an x at the top corner of the browser window, at the swiping away of a social media app. It's a privilege that comes at too high of a cost for the other to bear on their own. It's a privilege Jesus didn't even consider grasping but gave up to come dwell with us.

Love means being inconvenienced. It means entering the pain of others and holding space, not rushing to solutions or placing blame or figuring out happy endings. It means sitting in the discomfort of unresolved issues and somehow still holding hope for a future, for redemption, even when it seems impossible.

Love means showing up, speaking up, and sticking around when it not only costs us inconveniences but even more so when it costs us our reputation, our relationships, our time, our energy —possibly even our lives.

When we lay down our privilege, we follow in the way of Jesus, who broke down all barriers, who laid down every privilege He had, who took on all the pain, all the sadness, all the grief, all the death and said, "It is finished."

We can make the choice to lay down our privilege like Christ did. We don't have to know what to do next. We can pay attention to the pain around us, listen to those who are crying out, and pray for God to make all things right again.

PRAYER

God, I'm overwhelmed by what's happening around me. There are so many people whose lives are falling apart, so much unfairness and injustice, and I don't even know where to begin to pray. The only words I have now are these: Lord, have mercy. Christ, have mercy. Lord, have mercy. Come, Lord Jesus. Amen.

In every high and low,
every mountaintop and valley
and pathway in between,

God's love has proven constant and sure.

Seasons change,
but He remains.

—KAITLYN BOUCHILLON

Day 37

the truth about church hurt

And let us consider how to stir up one another to love and good words, not neglecting to meet together, as is the habit of some, but encouraging one another, and all the more as you see the Day drawing near.

Hebrews 10:24–25 ESV

I've been told more than once that I have a childlike faith. I rarely question God. I seek silver linings. I trust His plans for my life—which are usually quite different from my own—knowing some details may take years to unfold and I can only see the drive, not the destination. Childlike faith isn't only for those with a smooth, untroubled church history (and honestly, who has that?). It's for everyone.

But what do you do when pain comes from the place that should bring you comfort? How do you handle it? Some turn away in anger while others retreat like wounded animals, hiding to lick their wounds. Neither is a healthy response for you or for the body of Christ, His church. Instead, I've learned that church is composed of people—human, fallible, sons and daughters of Adam, sinners—people like me. Although I know our purpose as Christians is to glorify God and point a fallen world to the cross, some days I succeed and other days I fail quite spectacularly. So is it right for me to expect more from others?

Thankfully, the Bible doesn't shy away from examples and stories of human brokenness while still showing God's redeeming work. King David did terrible things—committing adultery with Bathsheba and then arranging to have her husband killed by placing him in the heat of battle—and yet the Bible calls him "a man after [God's] own heart" (Acts 13:22). The apostle Paul went from persecuting the early disciples of Jesus to dedicating his life to the spread of Christianity and writing much of the New Testament. Even the best "sin and fall short of the glory of God" (Rom. 3:23).

I also haven't been immune to failing or to experiencing the failings of others in the church, but I've found my way through and emerged on the other side. I once watched as my church family divided in half. That our once-unified body of believers would never worship together again was almost more than I could bear. My husband and I weren't sure we still wanted to be at our church, but we didn't feel led to go anywhere else.

The following Sunday we moved from our usual pew on the second row to sit near the back of the building. I cried through most of the service and left before it ended. Some of my dearest friends stood on the other side of the division. It took time, patience, and hard conversations, but those relationships are now stronger than ever, and I know those forever-friendships can withstand fire.

We will never attend a church of perfect people, because there are no perfect people. We will disappoint our brothers and sisters in Christ, and they will disappoint us too. Thankfully, we are not told to put our faith in other people but in a pure and holy God who will never leave us or fail us. The New Testament tells us to come together in worship, many parts uniting together as one body of believers. Remember: hurts caused by the church are a result of human sinfulness, not God's failure. If we forgive people and hold strong to Jesus, we can live with a clearer perspective and realistic expectations about people and the church. And we can still have childlike faith, knowing that God is redeeming His body, His bride, until Christ returns.

PRAYER

Lord, we are Your people, and the church is too. Yet we are all just that—people. Humans who are nowhere near perfect, sinners who are doing our best. But You are perfect. You are faithful and holy. You redeem the broken; You don't cause the breaking. Remind me of this when the wounds of church sting. You will never turn me away. Amen.

Day 38

when mothering is just too hard

> Two people are better off than one, for they can help each other succeed.
>
> Ecclesiastes 4:9 NLT

Last week my husband and our youngest daughter were sick, which meant the full load of carrying our family fell on me. I have a very involved and load-sharing husband, so the fact that he was down for the count all week was overwhelming. My kids hadn't all been back at school for a full week yet. Work deadlines were looming. The laundry was in falling-over piles around the house. There were no dishes in the cupboards, as they were all in the dishwasher (clean) and piled in the sink and on the counter (dirty). The coffee machine stopped working. And on the day that broke me, my daughter threw up on me.

That night I loaded up my other two kids in the car and we went to my mom's house. She put out a small swimming pool on the front lawn, put two pizzas in the oven, and listened to me talk. And talk. And talk. Then she sent me to the mall to replace the favorite pink T-shirt I had been wearing when my daughter threw up on me.

That was all it took to reset my mind and heart. That was love. That was being seen. That was a cool drink on a hot day. That was comfort.

That day, mothering was just too hard for me to do alone for one more minute. So I stopped trying and brought in help, because it's been my experience that two are indeed better than one.

Maybe it's a moms group at your church or your best friend or your neighbor. Wherever you find it, find a person.

We need backup. Encouragers. Help.

We weren't meant to mother alone.

PRAYER

God, help me just breathe for one minute. Breathe. In and out, deep and slow, one breath at a time. I am aching to be seen, heard, loved, and helped. Today, mothering just feels like too much, and I need the comfort of another person. Lord, bring me that person. I don't want to—I can't—mother alone. And if there's not such a person right now, be that person for me, God—the One I can lean on, cry to, laugh with, trust in, and be encouraged by. Thank You for always being in my village. Amen.

Day 39

hope that
doesn't disappoint

And not only that, but we also rejoice in our afflictions, because we know that affliction produces endurance, endurance produces proven character, and proven character produces hope. This hope will not disappoint us, because God's
love has been poured out in our hearts through the Holy Spirit
who was given to us.

Romans 5:3–5 CSB

His hand reaches out for mine on top of the sheets. And we
hold on tight. That grip that says, "Please don't let me go. If you
let go, I may fall." I lay my head on my pillow, wondering what
happened to the now-I-lay-me-down-to-sleep kinds of prayers.

When did life twist to need these hopeless prayers of crying
out and pouring out and wringing out our hearts together in the
dark? *When did we first notice just how small we are?*

His words get caught behind the lump in his throat. He loses
his balance. He pauses and presses on, laying all of it down on
a three-hundred-thread-count altar. Our grip tightens.

I whisper ancient words, imprinted on my heart in deep red
letters: "Suffering produces patience, patience produces character, and character produces hope. And hope does not disappoint us . . ."

I know and believe the words to be true, but logic gets in the way every time. It causes me to hesitate. And I breathe fearful and disappointed words into the night.

"Hope is always about what isn't," I say.

"It is always about what's missing," I mutter.

We sink to our knees and whisper timid words that ache with barrenness and emptiness and grief over what we've lost.

And then, weaving its way through my accusations, silently and gently squeezing in, just in time, the word *yet* falls from heaven and slips into place on this altar.

This word finds its way through a small space between our tightly clasped hands. It adds itself, completing and changing the meaning, filling our hearts with truth and overflowing them with hope.

In that instant I say and know the truth: Hope is not about what isn't. Hope is always about what isn't *yet*.

We sink to our knees and whisper timid words because of what isn't *yet*. In moments where we trudge through life between a weathered cross and a not-yet-empty tomb, hope brings us to our knees.

Hope causes us to lay our quivering and undone hearts on makeshift altars in the night. When I stumble over disappointments in the dark and feel swept away in hopelessness, even then it is hope that causes me to cry out to the One who is faithful despite my chronic faithlessness.

Our situation hasn't changed, but on our altar we've shifted our grip. No longer holding on for dear life, together we hold fast to the One who gives life. We have again put our hope in Him. We send forth heavy sighs of hope for unknowns that are yet to be.

And though we don't yet see it, our hands and hearts are open to receive this hope that does not disappoint.

PRAYER

Lord, please don't let me go. If You let me go, I may fall. There's this terrifying space that I'm in and have no control over, and it's building fear in my soul. So I come to You knowing that hope will not disappoint—Lord, I'm counting on it. I'm counting on You for that which produces hope. Hope for what isn't . . . yet. In Your name, Jesus, amen.

Day 40

why our tears are like seeds

Those who plant in tears
 will harvest with shouts of joy.
They weep as they go to plant their seed,
 but they sing as they return with the harvest.

Psalm 126:5–6 NLT

The other day I held a seed on the tip of my finger and studied it in the sunlight. The shape felt so familiar, but I couldn't quite place it. Then I read Psalm 126:5–6, and I realized that seeds are shaped remarkably like tears.

I thought then of how years ago I was given a packet of seeds at a local farm. I tucked them away in my purse with the best of intentions, but I never released them. So I never saw any growth or fruit from them in my life. I wondered if the same might be true of my tears, the ones I so valiantly resist. Perhaps crying is actually a lot more like planting, like the farmer dropping the seeds into the earth.

Maybe I resist the letting go because I know what happens next. There will be dark and dirt. There will be ugliness before loveliness. There will be little control. There will be waiting and watching. There will be the vulnerability of hope.

But it takes all these things for the becoming to happen. For the tiny seed, the little tear—so fragile—to transform itself into something strong and wild and capable of pushing through to the surface, to do whatever it takes to find the light again. And there comes that day when this happens. I see it even now beneath the bird feeder: a few green strands lifted boldly to the sky. "We are here," they say. "We have overcome."

New life. Growth. Good things. Harvest with shouts of joy.

I'm facing some struggles in my life, and this gives me comfort. Because I want to know that what I may cry about today could be what I rejoice over tomorrow. I want to know that there is a purpose in what I can't see or understand yet. I want to anticipate the yellow sunflower on the table or the sweet apple on my lips.

Maybe you are feeling this way too. If so, let's walk together into the fields with Jesus. Let's take the seeds from the places we hide them and watch them fall. Let's dare to believe that our tears are not really about an ending but instead, somehow, a beginning. And there is beauty coming.

PRAYER

Lord, may what I cry about today be what I rejoice over in time. May I trust that there is a purpose in what I can't yet see or understand. May I dare to believe my tears are not about an end, but somehow about a beginning. Amen.

tired of being scared?

So be strong and courageous! Do not be afraid and do not panic before them. For the Lᴏʀᴅ your God will personally go ahead of you. He will neither fail you nor abandon you.

Deuteronomy 31:6 NLT

You feel a rush of anxiety at what God is asking you to do. You think you lack the courage to take the next step. It sounds like too much for the little bit of brave you can muster.

Courage and perseverance have been themes throughout most of my life. Friends come to me seeking the courage they need to do the next thing. And I admit, I've pushed through and done major things in my life scared, not feeling very brave. But the secret I know is that obedience to God's direction in my life takes over when fear is present.

I cofounded (in)courage more than ten years ago, with a focus to give women the courage to live out their calling in Jesus. Led by the Holy Spirit, I started my own marketing company. I am creating a hobby farm with my family when I've only known life in the suburbs. All because I choose to walk in obedience to God's voice, not because I'm brave.

The Israelites tested the Lord while they were in the wilderness, saying, "Is the Lord going to take care of us or not?" (see Exod. 17:7).

When you and I are scared, I've learned we are really asking God this question: "Is Jesus going to take care of us?"

But when we ask that, we may already be afraid He won't. We worry and wonder, then we start to complain and wander.

Right before Joshua leads God's people into the promised land, Moses tells him that God will fight the battle, God will defeat the enemy, God will win the war, and God's people will possess the promised land. "Be strong and courageous, do not be afraid or discouraged, for the Lord your God will be with you wherever you go."

The key is to know the outcome before the battle. The reason Joshua, the Israelites, and you and I can be strong and courageous is because God keeps His promise that "the LORD your God will personally go ahead of you. He will neither fail you nor abandon you" (Deut. 31:6 NLT).

How was Joshua supposed to change his fear into strength and courage? Because God told him He would be with Israel and go ahead of them and fight all their battles. God told Joshua that He would not fail or forsake him.

The truth of God's word changed the reality and enabled Joshua to overcome fear. The truth led to courage.

Your bravery comes from truth and the ability to listen to God's voice and obey Him.

PRAYER

I need Your courage today, Lord. I'm scared and feeling small, and I need the bravery from Your truth to fill my heart and soul. I'm listening for Your voice, choosing to obey, and stepping forward in faith because I know the outcome before the battle. You will never fail me. Thank You for so faithfully keeping Your promises, God. Amen.

for when you struggle

Again, the kingdom of heaven is like a merchant looking for fine pearls. When he found one of great value, he went away and sold everything he had and bought it.

Matthew 13:45–46

I don't often wear pearls.

But when I do, I remember the struggle.

My husband gave me a beautiful strand of pearls during a hard season of life. It was a lavish gift for a sweatpants-wearing mom who hadn't left the house in weeks. Our third baby was born prematurely and spent the first months of life tethered to a heart monitor.

There was a new job, a new baby, a new set of challenges, a new season to navigate. And it all made me feel very old (and tired).

The day he brought the wrapped pearls home was the first day we attempted to get me out of the house. I laughed at the gift because they seemed so inappropriate for my dirty hair and weary body. But my sweet husband was determined to celebrate the new things in our lives, even though some of them were hard.

He carefully fastened the lustrous strand around my neck, and I traded my T-shirt for a dressy top. We loaded up the baby and her siblings, the medical gear, and the diaper bag, and drove the two short miles to our favorite restaurant.

Within a few minutes of sitting down, the waiter accidentally dumped the pitcher of sweet tea into my new diaper bag just as a terrible stomach bug was beginning in my preschool son. I carried him to the bathroom, where he got very sick. I propped open the door and tried to wave down a waiter to grab my husband, who was busy mopping up tea, jiggling a fussy baby, and regretting the whole idea.

We left the restaurant before we even ordered—a sad, soggy, stinky mess. We had a puker in the car and a fragile newborn. It was the car ride of nightmares.

I laughed and cried in my pearls the two miles back home.

Every time I see those pearls hanging in my jewelry box or around my neck, I remember that night. The irony of the pearls and the puke weren't lost on me.

But it took a while for me to remember how pearls are formed.

Pearls are created in oysters due to an irritant, usually a grain of sand. Grit. Pearls are the outcome of struggle. They are rare and priceless, unique and treasured. They are a product of irritation and are created as a defense against something that is hard, something that doesn't belong.

A pearl is a product of suffering. It is a healed wound.

And it takes perseverance and grit to produce anything.

Life is filled with struggle. But the hardship and trials are not wasted. Our struggle is irritating and annoying. Sometimes it's heartbreaking and horrible. But it's producing something good within us.

I don't know what your struggle is today or what it will be tomorrow.

Struggle is a part of living, but when we know we are producing something good, it helps us through it.

So put your pearls on, girl, and thank God in the midst of it. Something good is coming.

PRAYER

Even when everything seems to be going awry, God, I see You. I see beauty right in the middle of the hard things, the messiness, the aching, and the fear. Lord, I am clinging to the hope that something good is coming, that something good will be produced from the grit and struggle, that there will be treasure to behold after this hardship. In Your name, God, amen.

Day 43

when grief sneaks up on you

The LORD is near the brokenhearted;
he saves those crushed in spirit.

Psalm 34:18 CSB

The sleepover came to an end as my friend arrived to pick up her kids. With backpack in one hand and balloon in the other, her youngest flew out my front door. Immediately that balloon got caught in a gust of wind, making us laugh. But suddenly it burst!

One second the pink balloon had been dancing along the grass of our front yard and the next it had exploded into pieces of plastic, victim of a too-sharp blade of grass. Stunned, the adults shook our heads as our kids began crying. Who would've guessed that grass could be so dangerous?

Later, as I picked up toys and tossed sheets into the laundry, I thought about how that front-yard explosion was a little bit like grief, how something seemingly innocent can shatter our peace and bring us to tears. It reminded me of how grief can sneak up on us, biting out of the blue, striking with no warning.

Just like children playing with balloons know to look out for lightbulbs or cat claws, when you've experienced a loss, you know to anticipate deeper grief at certain times. Holidays, anniversaries, firsts or lasts—all these are hard to handle when you're doing it in the aftermath of a death, divorce, lost job, or broken relationship. But at least we can see these coming. It's the supposedly harmless blades of grass—the song on the radio, the turn of phrase only that person used, a movie you watched together, a simple question from a neighbor—that really get us.

When that happens, we can be tempted to feel shame. *I shouldn't be so upset. It's not a big deal. I should have it together by now. It shouldn't still bother me so much.* But grief doesn't follow a timeline—or really any rules at all. And nobody has the right to expect us to grieve a certain way—not even ourselves!

So the next time your heart is stabbed with something as innocent-looking as the grass in my front yard, give yourself some grace if it hurts. Take a deep breath, take some time, take the kindness and consolation that others offer.

And remember that God promises to be with the broken-hearted. Period. No restrictions or expiration dates. No exclusions or requirements. Just love and comfort—promised for and offered to you, no matter what breaks your heart this time.

PRAYER

Lord, sometimes when I least expect it, grief sneaks up and startles me to the core. The triggers have no warning, and my heart nearly can't take it. The pain feels so raw and recent; it takes my breath away and leaves me shaking. God, be near. Be with me. When my heart is broken and grief has shocked me yet again, meet me there with kindness, with Your love, comfort, and perfect peace. Amen.

let's pave a better future

In reply Jesus said: "A man was going down from Jerusalem to Jericho, when he was attacked by robbers. They stripped him of his clothes, beat him and went away, leaving him half dead. A priest happened to be going down the same road, and when he saw the man, he passed by on the other side. So too, a Levite, when he came to the place and saw him, passed by on the other side. But a Samaritan, as he traveled, came where the man was; and when he saw him, he took pity on him. He went to him and bandaged his wounds, pouring on oil and wine. Then he put the man on his own donkey, brought him to an inn and took care of him. The next day he took out two denarii and gave them to the innkeeper. 'Look after him,' he said, 'and when I return, I will reimburse you for any extra expense you may have.'

"Which of these three do you think was a neighbor to the man who fell into the hands of robbers?"

The expert in the law replied, "The one who had mercy on him."

Jesus told him, "Go and do likewise."

Luke 10:30-37

125

It was another routine pickup after school. I was waiting for my son and chatting with another Indian mom, when suddenly she broke down in tears. Her son, I found out, was being bullied at school, and kids were making fun of his homemade Indian food. As we talked, my own painful memories as a schoolgirl flooded in. I, too, used to bring rice and dal for lunch and was ostracized for it. Every day was the same: an empty lunch table with children pointing and laughing. I will never forget that kind of shame, and I certainly didn't want this boy to go through the same things I did.

The next week, my husband and I scheduled a meeting with the school principal to talk about what policies they had in place for racial bullying. We even joined a committee to confront racial discrimination. Procedures were created to handle these situations and to better care for kids who had been victimized. It was a start.

It's easy to think that racism isn't the same as it was thirty years ago, but not much has changed. The same cycle of prejudice and rejection continues, and I must play a vital role in breaking that cycle. If I don't want the pains of my past to be the problems of someone else's future, I need to help change our future.

In Luke 10:25–37, the good Samaritan finds a hurting man on a dangerous road, picks him up, and takes care of him. The Samaritan hadn't caused the problem, but he was part of finding the solution. The road that this beat-up man was traveling on was dangerous, and even though the good Samaritan didn't cause the danger or any of the harm that came to the man, it didn't mean he couldn't be part of making a better path for the future.

As believers, we are called to do the same. We must take care of one another, despite the pains we've experienced (and perhaps even because of them), so that those who come after us can travel down a much better road than we did.

PRAYER

Thank You, Lord, for the times I've been taken care of. Help me to recognize and step into circumstances that allow me to care for someone else and in doing so to pave the way for those who will come after me. Amen.

God promises to be
with the brokenhearted.

Period. No restrictions or expiration dates.

No exclusions or requirements.

Just love and comfort—

promised for and offered to you,

no matter what breaks your heart this time.

—MARY CARVER

Day 45

the start of something beautiful

This is what the LORD says—
who makes a way in the sea,
and a path through raging water, . . .
"Do not remember the past events,
pay no attention to things of old.
Look, I am about to do something new;
even now it is coming. Do you not see it?
Indeed, I will make a way in the wilderness,
rivers in the desert."

Isaiah 43:16, 18–19 CSB

It had never occurred to me *before* it happened that *when* it happened, I would be sad. I simply wasn't prepared for the call from my doctor, even though I had been aware of changes in my body for years. My tears were as bewildering as the news.

I may have experienced uncharacteristic mood swings, changes in skin texture, occasional hot flashes, and disrupted sleep, but how in the world could I possibly be *post*-menopausal when I still had the joy of a regular cycle? And yet, just becoming aware of my test results seemed to flip a switch. Within days of the phone call it seemed as if I traded the trim body of my youth for Mrs. Doubtfire's lumpy fat suit. Soon after, my monthly visitor stopped dropping by. I barely recognized myself in the mirror.

I hadn't anticipated a profound sense of loss that would accompany the "change." Though we had decided years earlier not to have more children, learning I couldn't was different. The thing that makes me most thankful that I'm a woman—the miracle no man has ever known and the thrill I've known three times over—could never happen again. I hadn't expected to grieve; on the contrary, in my youthful naiveté I thought I would only be *happy* when I reached menopause. What was going on?

It's a big deal when a girl starts her period. We say, or at least think on some level, that she's become a *woman*. So, when this season is over, is she no longer a woman? Does she become something else? That's silly, of course, but it still felt like a significant part of my life was over. I found myself feeling somehow less-than, maybe even old and irrelevant. We celebrate the change from girl to woman, but no one ever told me menopause might bring mourning. Always one to see the bright side and silver linings, I was confounded by my emotional response. Hormones might just be little devils.

When the shock of the call faded, I began to hear from the Lord. If menopause is the ending of one thing, might it also be the beginning of something else? Could what felt like a death sentence (to my womb at least) actually be a proclamation of new life, the genesis of a fresh season?

God, in His infinite kindness, sent a special seventy-eight-year-old friend to encourage me. "Do you realize if you've gone through these changes, you're one of the lucky ones? Not everyone makes it. Your mama didn't. What you have is today, and something beautiful can be made of it."

Though I hardly think the words in Isaiah 43 were written to menopausal women, they give me such hope and point me to a God who already knows my feelings and needs. They remind me not to fixate on the past but to look to my future with hope! God is always at work, and He wants me to live out my kingdom purpose in every season. He promises something new, even now. He always makes a way. And He wants me to live with eyes wide open.

My experience makes me want to seek out women a few steps ahead of me to learn what might come in the future and women a few steps behind me to offer the benefit of what I've already learned. I will be intentional, bold, and brave, pursuing friendships rooted in mutual love and service to one another. What a beautiful redemption of loss—to give from my void and abundance, to help prepare others for the unexpected.

Are you willing to join me?

PRAYER

God, if this is the end of one thing, could it truly be the beginning of another? I know You are always at work and that You always make a way. This feels like grief mingled with anticipation, and I'm going to need Your grace to make it through. Give me the courage to share my experience with others, to ask about their experience, and to be intentional, bold, and brave. Amen.

Day 46

learning from job loss

You intended to harm me, but God intended it for good to accomplish what is now being done, the saving of many lives.

Genesis 50:20

In my twelfth year as a journalist, I hit a big bump in my career. When the dust settled, I didn't have a job. *My* job, as I saw it, was given to someone else. And I was stunned. Devastated. Shell-shocked. In less than a year, however, I realized that losing that high-profile newspaper position—the only career downfall I'd ever experienced—turned out to be one of the best things that ever happened to me.

Instead of weeping and raging at myself and at God, I should have thanked God for being right there in the middle of it. Even better, He was ahead of it.

That low point led me to a high calling, my next position—teaching newspaper reporting and editing to eager graduate and undergraduate students on a large university campus. There I was forced to dig deep—to stir in my soul enough humility to learn how to teach.

And teach well.

That work forced me to learn to listen, but also to learn empathy, patience, clarity, order, dignity, self-control, prudence, integrity, passion—and to change lives while God changed mine. Newspaper work can stir up such gifts, I'm sure. But to

131

be honest, I never sought such virtues day after day until I stood in a classroom to teach.

I still thank God for allowing this unexpected journey, for turning what appeared to be bad into something far better than I ever imagined. I laugh to think how teaching forced me to learn public speaking—something I thought I hated. But I also was blessed to learn how to lead and facilitate workshops and seminars, all skills I routinely use in my life now as a Christian author. Even more, I reach far more people for the Lord in this, the "second stage" of my work life.

At first, I couldn't see any good in the bad. Most of us can't. But today, if you're smack in the middle of one of life's curveballs, catch it. Then bless God's Spirit by thanking Him for sending it your way. Know, as Joseph did in today's Scripture reading, that what life intends for evil, God will turn into good—for "the saving of many lives" (Gen. 50:20). And that is good—good enough for our thanks.

PRAYER

God, bring me to a place where I can give You thanks for allowing this unexpected journey. I'm not ready to be fully grateful yet, and I can't see the whole picture of what You're doing in this situation. But help me catch this curveball and thank You for it anyway, trusting that You will do good even in this. Amen.

the truth about loneliness

I am the one who answers your prayers and cares for you.

Hosea 14:8 NLT

Without question, the emotion that most consistently brings me to the very fringes of myself is not frustration, not anger, but garden-variety loneliness. For me, *this* is the root of all the others. The belief that I'm alone in the world, that no one has my back, has the power to crank my emotional equilibrium left of center.

As an introvert, it seems like I should be immune to loneliness. Give me a free day, and I'll scoop it up and steal away alone.

But there's a big difference in *being* alone and *feeling* forgotten or unseen.

In recent years I've faced this struggle more than ever before. I don't understand why God allows it. Shouldn't my faith be all the protection I need against this peril?

Two days ago, I finally recognized the power Satan has over me in this area. I hand him this weapon, and he finds it quite effective. If he can convince me I'm alone in the world, I willingly fork over a portion of my holiness, no questions asked. He fuels my pain as I lash out or become withdrawn or paranoid. He greases the rails of vindictiveness, and I ride. He double-binds me to myself—a guaranteed recipe for disaster.

This web widens, my fragility dangling more precariously in the balance with each silky loop. I circle back, telling myself I'm all I've got. *Buck up. Better get used to it. Who needs them, anyway?*

Friends, I wish I could tell you loneliness is a lie, the economy of the enemy dealing empty hands with dead eyes. But I keep watching the way God scoops me out of these valleys, and I can't find a way around it.

Dietrich Bonhoeffer writes in *The Cost of Discipleship*, "It is Christ's will that [man] should be thus isolated, and that he should fix his eyes solely on Him."

That is where my pitiful humanity wrecks this gift of loneliness. Over and over, rather than fixing my eyes on the One who loves me best, I frantically scan the horizon for a jeans-and-sneakers *person* to save me. I run to my husband or my mom. Affirmation is only a text message away. From the security of the school pickup line, from the comfort of my kitchen, I can yell for help and someone will throw me a float.

And yes, this is community. Yes, God loves His people *through* His people.

It is our unequivocal duty to love the lonely. We should be linking arms with the outcast, remembering that sometimes the outcast wears $200 jeans and drives an Audi. Sometimes the lonely sits in a nursing home, but she also sits next to us on the bleachers at gymnastics practice.

I feel like my relationships and my sanity might be protected if I learned to lean into God's presence rather than fumbling for the sick comfort of anger and self-pity.

I know God allows me to occasionally feel the burn of loneliness not only because He wants to rescue me but because He's called me into community, where others are lonely. Sometimes we need to feel pain to recognize pain.

So, if you're lonely, let me remind you that you're not alone. Alone doesn't exist within the bounds of God's love for you.

1. Dietrich Bonhoeffer, *The Cost of Discipleship* (New York: Simon and Schuster, 2012), 94.

The truth about loneliness is that it brings us to the edge of ourselves, which is actually the goal. Refuse to wrestle this gift from the Giver. Hold it as an opportunity to be cared for by the only One who *really* can. Let Him heal you. Then bear your scars as holy tattoos connecting you to the rest of His kingdom, marking you as the healed.

PRAYER

Jesus, I am so thankful that alone doesn't exist within the bounds of Your love for me. I want to choose to hold my pain as an opportunity to be cared for by You, the only One who really can. Over and over, help me hand You my loneliness and bear my scars as holy tattoos, witnesses to Your healing love. Amen.

Day 48

seasons change, but he remains

You go before me and follow me.
You place your hand of blessing on my head.

Psalm 139:5 NLT

Several years ago, I taped four pieces of paper with a Scripture verse on each one to my bedroom door. The pages are worn thin now, curling at the corners and faded from sunlight streaming through the window.

Over the years I've combined the verses into a short statement. Every morning I repeat the phrase as I reach for the doorknob and begin the day. It goes like this:

I can trust everything He does, for He goes before me and behind. I am merely a moving shadow, and all my busy rushing ends in nothing. My only hope is found in Him.

I said it this morning, and I'll say it again tomorrow. Through the highest of highs and the lowest of lows, these words of truth have been a constant and a comfort.

When I don't understand and I can't see what's coming next, I can trust everything God does (Ps. 33:4).

When I feel unsure and alone, He goes before me and behind (Ps. 139:5).

When I'm overwhelmed, God gently says it's my heart that He wants, not my performance or a completed to-do list (Ps. 39:6).

When I'm worn out or searching for a light in the darkness, God is my hope (Ps. 39:7).

I may not know what will greet me on the other side of the door, but I believe Truth not only walks with me but prepares and redeems all at the same time.

God goes before me to make a way and clear a path. He sticks with me, a constant friend and guide. And He comes behind me, redeeming all things for good even when I can't see it just yet.

In every high and low, every mountaintop and valley and pathway in between, God's love has proven constant and sure. Seasons change, but He remains, and so I repeat the phrase and hold on to hope, trusting the unknown of the future to the God I know is authoring its pages.

PRAYER

I can trust everything You do, God, for You go before me and behind. I am merely a moving shadow, and all my busy rushing ends in nothing. My only hope is found in You. No matter the season or circumstance, You remain. Help me to keep believing. Amen.

Day 49

when you're in the presence of grief

Rejoice with those who rejoice; mourn with those who mourn.

Romans 12:15

If I look around me now, it would seem as though all is well with the world. Of course, there *are* pockets and moments of all-is-well. There are still birthdays and weddings and babies' first steps to mark with confetti and hundreds of pictures. There are victories from addictions and dreams lived out to be celebrated. There are simple joys to savor, like eating dinner with the family around the dining table on a regular Wednesday night and the peace of a quiet home once everyone goes to bed.

There are all those things and the sun that shines, and yet they're not enough to balance the scale of grief and joy.

The weight of my friend losing her husband at too young of an age, the weight of those who have been taken advantage of by people with power and money, the weight of those who have been silenced and devalued—these lie heavy on my heart, and grief fills every inch of me. I know joy and hope are always found in God, and yes, I know He is good and sovereign, but right now I ache. I sit in silence while my heart screams, wishing we still practiced lament with sackcloth and ashes instead of putting on a brave face.

It isn't proper to be sad in our culture and in our churches. We are so quick to say our "at least" statements, so uncomfortable with what we cannot fix. We try to patch truths about God onto open, bleeding wounds with good intentions to get to hope, but we don't linger and mourn. We so fear the overwhelming darkness of grief, afraid of being swallowed by it, that we rush through and try to skip over the discomfort.

It seems to go against our nature to grieve communally and publicly, to mourn with those who mourn *in the very moment* they are mourning and to grieve with them as their grief stretches on.

We resist being present—as individuals and as the church—when faced with suffering, injustice, and death. But what if we didn't jump ahead to better times and made the conscious effort to be with those who are in pain? What if we let the tears flow and stopped putting a time limit on those who are grieving?

What if we, like Jesus, wept with our friends and entered into their loss, because every death is still a death, even when resurrection is around the corner?

I often hear this question from well-meaning people, including myself: "What can I do to help?" We see a problem in front of us and want to jump into action. We're not trying to be a hero, just a helper, but even so, I want to say, "You're missing the point. You're skipping the ache, wanting to wash it away, but can you stop, listen, and imagine how it might feel? Can you let your tongue and soul taste its metallic bitterness? Can you hold space for the rage, the tears, and the overwhelming sense of helplessness and hopelessness? Can you carry the weight of it all with them?"

It's not that we shouldn't plan and work toward hope and change. We should. But for now, look around you and listen to the weeping that is happening. Listen to the stories of pain, the stories of anger, the stories of injustice and death. Listen and bear it. Hold it and make space for it. Let your words be few and your presence be felt. And mourn with those who mourn.

PRAYER

God, there is so much pain and injustice all around me, and if I'm honest, it's easier to look away and pretend I can't see it all. But then I remember how You didn't look away from me, and instead You turned Your face toward me. Teach me to bear the weight, to see and listen, and to weep when others weep. Amen.

doubt in the wreckage

Are you the Messiah we've been expecting, or should we
keep looking for someone else?

Matthew 11:3 NLT

My son turned toward me with an empty drinking glass in hand,
ready to quench his thirst. Somehow the glass was let loose. It
slipped from his fingers like a ghost. I watched his eyes pop
like a puffer fish as the blue Ball jar transformed into a million
shards and flew across every inch of our slate tile kitchen floor.

Sometimes life feels like standing in a room surrounded by
sharp splinters and rough-edged remnants of what was.

There was a season when it seemed like everywhere I looked,
I saw those same shards of glass. I didn't know where to step or
how to move forward. If I'm honest, I doubted God's care and
closeness. I wondered why He didn't move the way I thought
He should. I wished He would just fix things and let me check
the mending. I wondered how I could keep offering the world
around me the message of living water when all the glasses I'd
carry it in kept breaking.

141

Throughout those months, God reminded me that I come
from a long spiritual line of those who question Him and struggle. Of those who were told to cast out their nets again in the
morning after the night left their hope empty and their hearts
weary. Of those who offered the little bread and fish they had,

then watched Him feed and fill a multitude. Of those who poured extravagant love at His feet and those who at first refused to let Him clean their feet. Of those who spent their lives preparing the way for a King they were devoted to, only to come to an end they didn't expect and to ask a question they never thought they would ask: "Are you the one we've been waiting for, or should we be waiting for someone else?"

Pick up one jagged piece and then another, He whispered back to me in the kitchen that day. *I'm not afraid of your doubt or the broken glass.*

Grace always weaves its way in and through the wreckage and the wounds. Doubt doesn't mean disbelief. The questions can lead us to God's presence. Our doubt can deepen our intimacy.

PRAYER

Lord, in my doubt, bring me closer to Your heart. Pick up my broken pieces and mend them while I trust in Your work and healing hands. Lead me to Your presence and peace. Amen.

my deathbed didn't scare me—healing does

> Have I not commanded you? Be strong and courageous. Do not be afraid; do not be discouraged, for the LORD your God will be with you wherever you go.
>
> Joshua 1:9

My deathbed didn't scare me. At fifteen, I was told I had a month to live. Yet dying didn't scare me.

After two years of misdiagnosis, I wasn't able to feed, bathe, or dress myself—basically, all I could do was roll over. I lost my home, my health, and my friends. Dying didn't scare me, but to be honest, it was mostly because I was too sick to notice. Thankfully, God guided my family and me through a miraculous healing journey. Four years after first getting sick with Lyme disease, toxic mold poisoning, and multiple chemical sensitivity, I'm well along the road to recovery and full healing.

But you know what? Healing intimidates me in ways illness never did. Healing means finally processing the fear and pain of what I went through. Healing has been hard, long, and in some ways perhaps even more painful than illness was. Healing means taking risks and doing things that two years ago—or even two months ago—would have sent me into a major health crash. Things like going for a walk, going to family worship

143

night, or eating a full meal. I couldn't have handled any of those things.

Healing means stepping into life again, even though so much has changed. Now I'm broken and scarred. I've seen awful parts of life no one should have to see. Healing means facing what I've been through so I can step into life again and facing the pain I ignored while in survival mode.

Healing is terrifying.

What if I stray from God when I'm no longer forced to turn to Him for every breath? What if my body falls apart again? What if the relationships illness stole and broke are forever irreparable? What if I fall when I take a step forward? What if I get broken again?

Maybe you can relate. I don't know what you're facing, what your past holds, or what you're healing from. Maybe it's a heartbreaking divorce. Maybe it's the death of a loved one. Maybe it's abuse from your past. Maybe, like me, it's a chronic illness or three. But chances are, there are parts of the healing that scare you, that intimidate you in ways nothing else has before, even the trial itself.

Many people may not understand how something so good and happy like healing can be so scary. But you are not alone. We have those like Joshua who have gone before us in faith, and I've found such encouragement from Joshua 1:9.

> Have I not commanded you? Be strong and courageous.
> Do not be afraid; do not be discouraged, for the Lord your
> God will be with you wherever you go.

There is so much truth in that one Scripture. But there is one part that has stuck out to me in this healing season—this healing battle. Joshua needed this encouragement not in the forty desert years but on the brink of the promised land.

Here's the thing: God didn't just say, "Be courageous." He gave a reason Joshua—and we—should be courageous. *For the Lord your God will be with you wherever you go.* You know how God was with you in the trial you're healing from? Well, He's going to continue to be with you in the healing and recovery process. We can be courageous because our Father is holding our hand. He walks with us in the pain of the past and in the promise, hope, and struggles of the future.

That isn't to say the healing won't be hard. Though Joshua entered the promised land in courage and victory, there were battles to be fought once the Israelites entered. Yet because God was with them, there was victory.

You are a warrior. Healing isn't easy, but in God's power and grace, you will make it. Stand in Him—there you can have courage. Because God is with you, you will have your own victory.

PRAYER

Father God, I'm scared to heal. I'm terrified of what comes next, of all that can go wrong, and of all the ways that my courage could fail me. But You have brought me this far, and I can trust You to bring me all the way into the promised land, because when You are with me, there is victory. I know it will continue to be hard, but I'm willing to fight because You have fought for—and won—me. In Your glorious name, God, amen.

braving our true identity

God said to Moses, "I AM WHO I AM. This is what you are to say
to the Israelites: 'I AM has sent me to you.'"

Exodus 3:14

As requested, I gave my name to the public service nutrition agent.
I could sense her shaming me for having another baby while on
public assistance. After recognizing my name from having received assistance the previous year, she paused and glared at me
with disgust. Her look of disapproval wrote me off as a stereotype
of codependence. Translation: *You should not be having babies
if you can't afford to care for them without public assistance.*

But I responded to her demeaning scowl with a confident,
giddy grin, unfazed.

What she did not know was that I felt fortunate to have birthed
another baby only eighteen months after our second child. At
face value, our circumstances were not the stuff that family-
growing dreams are made of. I was forty years old. I worked
part-time. My husband, in order to be a full-time graduate student, could not have a job. Thus, our family's income was almost
nonexistent.

But aren't we more than our circumstances, favorable or un-
favorable? When we understand the divine essence of who we
are, we know that it's not about our place or our circumstances
but about how we address ourselves.

The Hebrew word translated as "I Am" means "I exist" or "existence." So "I Am Who I Am" means "I exist as I am" or "I exist in my true nature."

When we understand God as the Infinite Being, we can see ourselves not as products of our past or present but as producers of our future. And we don't have to journey alone. We get to coauthor our own stories.

I am creative. I am courageous. I am more than my circumstances. I am more than what I seem. And most of all, I am with the great I Am.

PRAYER

Lord, when times are difficult, overwhelming, or sad, help me to remember that You, the great I Am, are always with me. Remind me of my true identity when labels are put on me by other people, when lies are spoken over me, and when circumstances determine to shake me. Amen.

Day 53

beauty in brokenness

The Lord is close to the brokenhearted
and saves those who are crushed in spirit.

Psalm 34:18

I talk often about how imperfect life is. With all the beautiful
photos we put up on Instagram, sometimes it's easy to think
that a person's life is perfect or charmed. And while I'm surrounded by so many blessings, I'm also surrounded by so much
brokenness.

I have a friend who is struggling with depression and a friend
who is facing infertility. Another friend was in a horrible car
accident, and the marriage of two close friends is crumbling
around them. Brokenness is everywhere.

Meanwhile, in my own life I'm caring for a seventeen-year-old
who still has to be diapered, fed, and given medication three
times a day. He is also tons of fun, super silly, and the best
snuggle bug, but the drain that comes from meeting his needs
day in and day out is real. Not to mention all the other responsibilities that fill up my days.

I look around me and I see all this brokenness, but what's
even harder for me to look at is the brokenness in my own heart.
I am self-centered, prone to fatigue, and sometimes discouraged.
I think I'm doing just fine, being productive and full of energy,
when all of a sudden I feel angry and resentful.

Isn't this the stuff of life? The comfort of the mundane can drive us to insanity. The joys of being a mother are overshadowed by feelings of failure. And the beauty of a new day is clouded by a long to-do list.

I am broken. I am needy. I can't fix myself. That's where I see the incredible beauty of God's grace. There is hope in that broken and needy place.

PRAYER

God, I am a broken person. Self-centered, needy, unable to fix myself, and I need You. We need You. Brokenness is everywhere. Send the hope that comes from Your heart to ours, and help me see the incredible beauty of Your grace right here, in the middle of the brokenness. Amen.

loving yourself matters

"Love the Lord your God with all your heart and with all your
soul and with all your mind and with all your strength." The
second is this: "Love your neighbor as yourself."

Mark 12:30–31

It was early in the new year when we threw a first-year party
for my son Ezra. Metallic streamers and three-dimensional gold
stars hung all over the dining room to celebrate. "Twinkle, twinkle little star, he's grown so much and come so far."

About twenty friends joined us that morning, and all our kids
were running amok around the house. Amid the mayhem right
there in the living room, a dear friend shared her pain. The joy of
the occasion couldn't prevent her hurt from breaking through. As
we drank coffee, my friend talked about the miscarriage she had
experienced earlier that year and how she still cried about it often.

How her husband was tired of her crying.

How she was going to start attending a support group to
seek comfort.

How she yearned for another child.

I just stood there, listening, the rest of the party fading away.
I grasped for words but none came, so I just hugged her tightly
and said that I loved her.

When the party was over and in the days that followed, I thought
about my friend. Not only did I think about her circumstances but

I thought about how in recent months I had not been the friend that she needed.

In Mark 12:30–31, Jesus shares the two most important commandments—to love the Lord your God with all your heart, soul, mind, and strength, and to love your neighbor as yourself.

I think we probably remember the "love the Lord" part. And we likely remember the "love your neighbor" part too. But that "as yourself" part—those are the words we forget.

That year, too many responsibilities prevented me from loving myself well. I over-yessed myself and ran on empty.

Consequently, when my friend had a miscarriage, I spoke with her and texted during those first hard weeks, but then I became distracted. Part of why I couldn't love her to the best of my ability was because I wasn't loving myself during that season.

Jesus knew that self-care isn't just about us. Loving ourselves has a positive ripple effect on our families, jobs, communities, and the world.

My prayer for you is that you embrace with renewed commitment Jesus's commandment to love your neighbor as yourself. Because in the end, most of us will do just that. And don't we all want our love to be big and bright?

PRAYER

Lord, I want to love my neighbor as myself, but it's hard when I struggle with loving myself at all. Give me the grace needed to see myself as worthy of love, care, and compassion. I want my love to be big and bright, to embrace Jesus's commandment with renewed commitment and a joyful heart. Help me to start with myself and then to love others from that place of love. Amen.

151

Day 55

if motherhood is hard,
you are not alone

You have searched me, LORD,
    and you know me.
You know when I sit and when I rise;
    you perceive my thoughts from afar.
You discern my going out and my lying down;
    you are familiar with all my ways.

Psalm 139:1–3

In the early days of motherhood, worn-out running shoes and a rickety double stroller held my sanity. Daily I tied up those laces like I was girding my flailing ability to mother. I strapped the toddlers into their seats and doled out snacks and sippy cups. Then I hoisted the baby into the apparatus attached to my chest. Tiny sun hat and pacifier—check. Burp cloth tucked in my back pocket in case the morning's projectile spit-up wasn't quite finished—check.

My feet pounded the pavement as I strained to propel the precious cargo forward. I pushed harder, trying to relieve the pressure that pressed from the inside. I was out of breath before I made it to the end of the block. The boys babbled to one another about kitties perched in picture windows and earthworms squished flat on driveways.

I battled my thoughts.

Just go home! You're sleep-deprived and out of shape. Turn on the TV for the kids and go back to bed. But then I'd hear, *No, you need this. Stay the course. You'll find your rhythm. Just breathe.*

As much as my legs hurt and my lungs burned, I had to keep going. I turned toward the foothills aglow with morning light and made my way to the quaint main street just coming alive. The baby kicked his legs and a tiny sock fell off again. I paused to pick it up, sip some water, kiss each toddler.

I kept pushing north until shops and crowds fell behind us. Historic bungalows and craftsman homes now lined the wide street. Ample sidewalks flanked each side. A tree overloaded with bright yellow blossoms popped glory against the blue sky.

I took a deep breath. Fresh air like soul medicine. The most peace I'd felt all week.

Motherhood comes to everyone differently. Some women dream of wrapping babies in pastel blankets from the time they are little girls, while others stumble upon motherhood in pink-line terror. Some moms never have a swollen womb but their hearts swell for children who need a home. Though our roads to motherhood vary, I believe one thing is the same: *being* a mom is never quite what we expected.

I never expected to have three boys in three and a half years. I never expected to go from a thriving career woman who felt sure in her abilities to a mom who felt ill-equipped to mother—a squishy, sleep-deprived shadow of my former self, whose felt purpose moved little beyond butt-wiper and milk machine.

Don't get me wrong. I loved my babies. I loved their satin skin and bald baby heads. I loved cuddling them in footie pajamas and singing countless refrains of "Jesus Loves Me." I loved each wobbly step and wonky first word.

153

But I never expected when people said motherhood was hard that the struggle would be so much greater than finding the right bedtime routine or getting a kid to eat green beans. My hunch is I'm not the only one who feels this way.

If you've ever whispered to yourself, *Being a mom is too much.* If you've ever locked yourself in the bathroom, crying tears for reasons you could not name. If you've ever loved your life yet desperately wanted an escape from it. If you've ever felt achingly alone though touched a thousand times by tiny hands every waking hour—you are not alone.

If you've ever longed for just one friend who gets it. If you've ever felt not cut out for it. If you've ever been convinced someone else would do it all better, hold it all together—you are not alone.

Sometimes in the flailing we just need to know someone sees us and understands. God sees you, friend. Always.

PRAYER

God, I'm overwhelmed by motherhood and the unexpected loneliness that comes with it. Everyone around me seems to be moving on with their lives, but I'm here doing the same day over and over again. Undo the lie that I'm alone in this and that no one understands me. Help me to reach out and ask for help when I need it and to believe that You really are with me in this. Amen.

When all the striving,
all the gifts, all the callings
and passions are set aside,
and when all that remains is only Jesus,

take heart.

You're not lost.
You're not without purpose.
Stay near and abide in Christ,
and that is enough.

—GRACE P. CHO

what you were made to strive for

Instead, strive for his kingdom, and these things will be given to you as well.

Luke 12:31 NRSV

I am an achiever.

This personality trait typically serves me well. If you ask me to do something for you, it's as good as done. If I set a goal, I actually take delight in working hard to exceed my own high expectations. I love work, which means I'm the kind of weird person who enjoys eight o'clock on a Monday morning in the same way that some people get excited about five o'clock on a Friday afternoon.

But like most personality types, there's a shadow side to mine. The problem? I take on more than I should. I say yes way too often. And I often live a half step away from burnout.

Even if you wouldn't describe yourself as an overachiever, I'll bet you know that draining feeling of burnout and overwhelm. You know how your schedule can fill up, even when you've tried to protect spaces on your calendar for refreshment and renewal.

No matter our personality type, it's so easy to find ourselves striving. There's constant pressure on us to strive because of the demands of everyday life.

We strive to meet deadlines. We strive to meet benchmarks and goals. We strive to teach our kids right from wrong. We strive to provide for our families, and we strive to support our friends.

At our best, we strive to do good in this world. At our worst, we strive to get ahead, get more followers, or achieve another level of success because we never feel satisfied with where we are.

Who else is tired of all the striving but feels like "If I don't do it, who will?"

My hand is raised.

One Sunday morning, while sitting under the steeple of our country church in Iowa, my eyes fell upon a striking verse in the Gospel of Luke. Here Jesus tells us what we should *really* be striving for.

"Instead, strive for his kingdom" (Luke 12:31 NRSV).

If you are a striver like me, Jesus is calling us to strive for this one thing alone! More of Jesus. More of His Spirit. More of His presence in our lives.

But this passage of Scripture contains more riches. In it, Jesus promises us that if we strive for His kingdom, everything else that's *truly* important "will be given to you."

This isn't the kind of striving we are used to in the hustle of our everyday lives. Let's not look at this kind of striving as pulling ourselves up by our bootstraps or trying to impress Jesus with what we can do.

Instead, this kind of striving is an arms-wide-open stance that says to Jesus, "I'm all yours."

As your day gets underway, there will be many people and projects that will ask something of you. You will be tempted to strive and hustle. With all the demands that will surely come your way, remember Jesus's command to "strive for his kingdom."

Let's strive for that one thing alone. That's all He is asking of us.

What a relief. What a Savior.

Jesus, I am all Yours. May I strive only for Your kingdom and resist the temptation to hustle and try to pull myself up by my bootstraps. May I stand with arms open and heart ready to hear from You alone. Amen.

huddled together

Two are better than one because they have a good reward for their efforts. For if either falls, his companion can lift him up; but pity the one who falls without another to lift him up. Also, if two lie down together, they can keep warm; but how can one person alone keep warm? And if someone overpowers one person, two can resist him. A cord of three strands is not easily broken.

Ecclesiastes 4:9–12 CSB

Our friend clutched the coffee cup, fingers intertwined, tears streaming down her face. The air sat heavy around the three of us, a silent vapor settling deep. As she tried to collect her thoughts, we listened.

"My marriage is crumbling. We aren't sleeping in the same room anymore. We've tried to hide it from our kids, our families, basically from everyone because we thought we could work through it by ourselves. That was a mistake. All that it's led to is isolation and loneliness. I can't do this anymore."

I sat stunned. My heart agonized at the bombshell she dropped. In that moment she didn't need either of us to give a hasty response or share five meaningful steps to heal her broken heart. There were no quick fixes or easy answers amidst the agony, but I could offer tenderness that receives grief with listening ears, that acknowledges the only remedy to her deep ache is to fall at the feet of Jesus—the Master Healer.

As I've fleshed out what it means to bear one another's burden in the context of community, a powerful visual has been imprinted on my heart.

Last year, disastrous hurricanes pummeled my beloved North Carolina coast. In the midst of mandatory evacuations, power outages, and devastating loss, many concerned animal lovers wondered how the free-roaming wild horses of the Outer Banks could survive.

My research revealed these majestic creatures have an incredible instinct for survival and protection. As they sense impending danger through a shift in air pressure, they don't exhibit a fight-or-flight response. Isolation is not in their nature. They seek out shelter together. They hunker down and huddle together. With their backsides to the wind, they protect one another from the damaging elements. Wild horses were created to weather life's most challenging storms together. It's woven into their very DNA.

Can you envision it? This beautiful picture of how we are called to protect and defend, to strengthen and solidify, to help and hold one another's burdens?

Huddled together face-to-face, backsides to the wind.

"I need you guys," our friend exhaled.

With our six hands clasped to form a cord not easily broken, we looked one another in the eyes. No one had the right words, but we knew the One who did. And as the storms of life continued to crash, we huddled together face-to-face with our Savior at the helm.

PRAYER

God, thank You for creating us for community so that we don't have to do this life alone. Weave me together with my friends, helping me to hold them up in Your strength when they need it and to lean into them when I need support and encouragement. Thank You for my friends and for Your friendship, God. Amen.

somehow there is still good

Every good gift and every perfect gift is from above, coming down from the Father.

James 1:17 ESV

My world came to a standstill the day my friend died.

I think if I'd looked out the window that August afternoon, everything would have been frozen in place. The trees, the wind, the sun—each of them paused mid-motion. At least, that's how it felt it should be. I did not see how the world could keep moving once her heart had stopped.

Tat Blackburn was twenty years old when the truck collided with her car on a rainy highway. She and her fiancé were driving from Saskatchewan back to Ontario through Wisconsin. They wanted to get deep-dish pizza in Chicago. He had proposed a few days earlier.

I had never heard the sound of a heart break until Tat died. Then I heard the sound often.

Over a thousand hearts shattered at her funeral. It was the largest funeral I'd been to, and when I stood to give my eulogy, I looked out at all the people who were impacted by her life. I was astonished. I hated the reality of having a funeral for my friend, but still, I was achingly proud of her.

My heart continued breaking—on her twenty-first birthday, on what should've been her wedding day, on regular days when I

161

wanted to take her out for cheesecake. Grief is like that—it pummels your heart again and again and again. I think loss leaves your heart black-and-blue and bleeding for a long time.

I once found myself sobbing in the smoothie section of the grocery store. Tat and I would always split Amazing Mango smoothies. I had forgotten about that until I saw the familiar yellow bottle in the grocery store fridge. Grief overcame me, and I burst into tears in the middle of the store. How could a *smoothie* contain so much joy and so much sadness?

But this is the tension I have found myself in daily: even in my insurmountable grief, there is good. There is always good because there is always God.

I think about Tat every day. I have come no closer to an answer for why she died. I am starting to think I will never know until I see her again. But I do have answers on other things: I believe that every good thing comes from God. And I believe that even in our heartache and devastation, God is always good.

I don't see Tat's death as good. It's awful and painful and wrong. But I see God's kindness and goodness through her death. In numerous ways, God has reminded me of His love and His tenderness. God's got Tat, and God's got me.

There is still good—even in sorrow. Because God is always good.

The night Tat died, Jesus gave me a dream. I saw her with Him.

She was wearing a gauzy white dress, and her hair was long and flowing even though she'd recently cut it. Her hand was entwined with His, and her facial expression was filled with a kind of adoration I had never seen here on earth.

Jesus was gazing down at her, delight pouring like sunshine from all of His facial features. I could feel the warmth radiating from Him, even though I knew I was not there with them.

Tat's smile extended, and she tilted her head back.

And then she laughed.

Jesus is with Tat. At the same time, He is with you and me— and let me tell you: even when nothing else around us is good, His presence in the midst of our deepest pain is a good gift indeed.

PRAYER

Lord, You are good, and Your presence is steady when life is incredibly painful. These words are not always a comfort, to be honest, but at times just reciting them can soothe my grief-stricken soul. You are still good. No matter what. Whether I understand my circumstances or not, when I cry out in grief, You are still good. Lord, help me lean into this truth when I really need peace to overwhelm my soul. In times of sadness, let me recall the good gifts You've given and see small pieces of goodness in the world. And when I'm just not okay, comfort me, Lord. Amen.

Day 59

it's all about perspective

"For my thoughts are not your thoughts,
neither are your ways my ways,"
declares the LORD.
"As the heavens are higher than the earth,
so are my ways higher than your ways
and my thoughts than your thoughts."

Isaiah 55:8–9

I love taking photos, and when editing them, I zoom in to see how clear the image is. It's my way of picking the best one. I was admiring the details on a photo one day when my husband came by. I asked if he could tell what it was. All you could see were thin black and red stripes, slightly curved, equally spaced, running diagonally. He had all kinds of interesting guesses but wasn't sure.

It's much easier to understand when we can see the whole picture, isn't it?

When we are in the midst of a difficult season, it's overwhelming because we can't see a way out or what the purpose is or when things will change. We just want to make sense of it all. But when we take a moment to remember Who is painting the picture, we can rest in that.

We are not in control. We have limits. God does not. And when we remember He is limitless, we know just how much we need Him.

When we let our own limited perspective get in our way, we miss Him in the midst. When we dwell on the outcome, we miss what He is doing in the now.

In Isaiah, we are reminded that God's ways and thoughts are beyond ours. There are things we just can't see or know.

He understands and He knows our circumstances. He is our Guide, as well as our Helper. He meets us right where we need Him, and He knows how it will all come together. There is a larger meaning to our journey, and nothing is ever wasted.

I know we can look back on things and see His hand at work, but I also understand how difficult it is at the time to get through a situation because we don't see the bigger picture.

Let me encourage you to hold on tight to faith as the story unfolds. Time will pass, and seeing things from God's planned perspective will be like seeing with new eyes.

I zoomed the image back out and it became clear to my husband what the image was. It was a beautiful red cardinal feather.

What a difference the proper perspective can make!

PRAYER

Lord, give me eyes to see with even a hint of Your perspective. Though the situation I'm in is confusing and unclear, I know it makes sense to You. And though it's not how I would choose to journey, I'm not the one in control. You are. You've painted the picture and now I need Your help to navigate the small part I am able to see. Guide me, God, and give me fresh perspective to see the bigger story in time. Amen.

when all you can do is pray

> In the same way the Spirit also helps us in our weakness, because we do not know what to pray for as we should, but the Spirit himself intercedes for us with unspoken groanings.
>
> Romans 8:26 CSB

As a mother with some children still at home and others who have left the nest, I've found it difficult not to feel responsible for the actions of my adult children. We're pleased—even proud—when they do good but feel a sense of blame when they don't. At least I do.

What can we do if we see our adult child traveling a path toward destruction? Some decisions are life-altering, multigenerational, take-no-prisoners kind of mistakes that affect everything and everyone they touch. It's like watching an avalanche in slow motion, and we feel helpless.

Too often I turn to prayer as a last resort, as an "I've done everything else I can do, so now I'll hand it over to God" alternative. But when you come to the end of yourself, you realize God is the only hope. He always has been. He hears us and He knows our needs.

Even when we don't know what or how to pray, the Holy Spirit intercedes on our behalf.

We are wired to safeguard our loved ones, to instinctively protect them from danger, heartache, and pain. But sometimes it's themselves they need protection from. What happens when we can't shield our adult child or when they won't listen? That's when we pray even harder.

I've learned that worry solves nothing, but prayer can change everything.

You and I cannot soften a hardened heart, but Jesus can.

You and I cannot heal a broken spirit, but Jesus can.

You and I cannot change a stubborn mind, but Jesus can.

You and I cannot see what the future holds, but Jesus can.

The God of the universe is strong enough to hold all things in place and to glue together the broken pieces of our hearts.

Do you carry heartache too heavy to bear? The popular saying "God won't give us more than we can handle" misses the point: He never intended for us to do it alone. Sometimes all we can do is pray. And that's enough.

PRAYER

God, whether I'm at the end of my rope or there's still a bit of length left, I'm coming to You now as my only hope. My heart is heavy as I think about my children, and I don't even know what to say. So I offer all I have—a silent prayer—trusting that Your Spirit will intercede on my behalf. Listen to my prayer, God. Amen.

rest and be the beautiful you

Come away by yourselves to a secluded place and rest a while.

Mark 6:31 NASB

The day had just started, but the whole week ahead already felt old. *I* felt old.

The sun was shining. The sky was blue. It was such a pretty day as I looked out the window over the kitchen sink.

I saw the beauty, but you know what? I didn't *feel* the beauty that was right in front of me. Have you ever had a morning like that—when the morning is still young, but you look at the week ahead and you already feel weighed down and tired?

What I needed was rest.

But the rest I needed wasn't just because my body was tired. I was weary in my heart and stressed in my soul. I needed emotional and spiritual rest.

Sometimes it's tempting for us to hide and stay invisible behind the busyness of taking care of others, rather than recognizing our need for beauty and joy. It may feel risky stepping out to be the beautiful person God created you to be. What has God put on your heart that would refill your tank so you can light up with joy and peace?

Whatever it is, nurture it with rest. Rest isn't doing nothing. It's blossoming in God's love by boldly moving to enjoy the things that help you experience that love. Rather than trying to fit into someone else's idea of beautiful, rest and be the beautiful, true you! It's easier to get pulled away by busyness and stress, but busyness takes a toll on all of us. We rush from one thing to the next, but the checklists never end. Unless we step away and allow God to restore us, we will become depleted and diminished in our capacity to feel our emotions and love others.

Though we may feel guilty, God tells us the truth: we are worth the rest and nourishment. What if God's plan for us is not to be more busy but to be more loved? Hear God whisper to you today, *You are beautiful to Me. Come away with Me and rest a while.*

Be kind to yourself and find a place for your weary soul to rest in His irrevocable love for you.

PRAYER

God, I need rest. Not just sleep or relaxation, but soul-deep rest. My heart is weary. The busyness is taking a toll, and I have heard You tell me to come away and rest. Please help me do just that in a way that works for where I am right now. I need more than a latte or a weekend at a spa. Meet me in the middle of my exhaustion, Lord. Restore me, nurture me, and fill me with Your irrevocable love. Amen.

Day 62

the goodness of God

This is why I wait upon you, expecting your
   breakthrough,
for your word brings me hope.

Psalm 130:5 TPT

With the state of the world, it's hard to wrap our minds around the goodness of God and suffering around the globe. The next level is trying to understand God's goodness in relation to our own hardships or those of our loved ones.

Context is key, and perspective is everything.

My life has been no walk in the park. I was born into hard circumstances. I was born into all manner of dysfunction and sinful living. I was neglected and abused. Trauma was my existence.

But God. He came in as the rescuer that He is and rescued me. He didn't rescue me *from* my circumstances as much as He rescued me *within* them. He saved my heart and soul and mind from the enemy. He saved me from myself. Where I am today is only because of His grace and mercy.

170

A friend recently told me that I had every reason to run from God, but I chose to run toward Him and let Him use my life for His glory. I cried tears of awe and gratitude. It was His goodness that drew me in when I was in college. It was His goodness that held me in hard times over the last two decades. It is His goodness that reminds me that He will continue to be faithful in the days ahead.

If I'm not vigilant, the noise and brokenness of this world can distract me from God's character. My focus can easily become fixed on everything that's wrong instead of the God that is right.

But there are a million and one ways that God displays His goodness. Psalm 130 highlights a few of them:

> Lord, if you measured us and marked us with our sins,
> who would ever have their prayers answered?
> But your forgiving love is what makes you so
>   wonderful.
> No wonder you are loved and worshiped!
>   (Ps. 130:3–4 TPT)

The very nature of God is holy and righteous, and He literally cannot be in the presence of sin. Then there's us, fallen humanity. When Adam and Eve sinned, it separated us from God's presence, but it never separated us from His love. The amazing thing about God is that He had a contingency plan. He had Jesus. Before He laid the foundations of the world, He knew we would go astray. And He made a way for us to be restored back to relationship with Him.

He bows down low to hear our prayers. And He always answers, although it may not be in our timing or the answer we wanted. He extends mercy to sinners and those that are working out their salvation. He forgives and He forgets.

> This is why I wait upon you, expecting your
>   breakthrough,
> for your word brings me hope. (Ps. 130:5 TPT)

His faithfulness is just that—faithful. He is the God who doesn't change. He is the same yesterday, today, and forever. His Word is flawless and speaks life to weary souls. It brings hope and breakthrough about the future. His kindness leads us to repentance, and His gentleness invites us to come boldly before His throne of grace. He would and did pay the highest price for our redemption.

When times get tough for me or for my community, I want to plant my feet firmly on the truth of God's Word and what I have experienced of Him.

I have experienced nothing short of God's unconditional love, extravagant grace, and unrelenting goodness. His goodness is real and steadfast. It's for me. It's for you. It's for the world.

PRAYER

Lord, thank You for Your faithfulness in my life. You are the same yesterday, today, and forever. I can trust You because You never change. Thank You for that gift! Help me run to You instead of away from You when things get tough. Amen.

how to heal a broken heart

He heals the wounds of every shattered heart.

Psalm 147:3 TPT

It was a Sunday morning at a retreat center in Texas. The morning light shone in perfectly on the communion table. A few dozen of us had gathered that weekend to seek refreshment in Jesus.

Up front stood Pastor Gordon.

As the service began, Gordon asked us to confront what felt shattered in our lives—broken relationships, broken dreams, broken hearts, even our own brokenness.

Then he paused, giving us time to consider questions like:

What heartbreak has shattered you to the core?

Does it feel like healing will never come?

What relationships or dreams have completely fallen apart for you?

His questions hung in the air for a long time. In the silence, I closed my eyes and thought about the emotional heartbreak caused by a friend's betrayal months earlier. Time is supposed to heal all wounds, right? But things weren't working out that way for me.

Maybe you know what that feels like.

Friend, imagine yourself sitting next to me, with the communion table set before us. Consider Gordon's questions, still hanging in the air.

You will likely answer his questions differently than I did. But perhaps Gordon can speak into your brokenness today, just as he did for me that morning.

Gordon spoke of the powerlessness we feel when everything falls apart, when our fragile lives look like they've crashed into a million little clay pieces—utterly unfixable. Then he knelt down in front of us and cupped his hands, as if he were scooping up all the broken pieces of our lives. He lifted his hands upward and spoke words I've not forgotten.

"I can't fix this," he said, cupping his hands toward God. "But can You? Can You do something with all these broken pieces?"

I believe with all my heart that God's answer is yes, based on His promise in Psalm 147:3 that He will heal your shattered heart.

It takes more than time to heal a broken heart, though. The paradox here is that it took brokenness to heal brokenness. It took Jesus—flogged, beaten, mocked, spit upon, and nailed to a cross.

Let's take our shattered hearts to that shattering on the cross. Jesus heals your wounds—not just with time but entirely with His own brokenness—to make you whole.

PRAYER

God, I can't fix this, but can You? I'm putting all the pieces before You and leaning hard on Your promise of healing what is shattered—lives, hearts, relationships. Take these pieces and make them new, Lord. Make them into something whole. I cling to You and wait on You, Jesus, to put them together. Amen.

174

ELIZABETH MANLEY

tethering our hearts to Jesus in loss

For I am convinced that neither death nor life, neither angels nor demons, neither the present nor the future, nor any powers, neither height nor depth, nor anything else in all creation, will be able to separate us from the love of God that is in Christ Jesus our Lord.

Romans 8:38–39

It was the spring of 2007, and I was a newly married twenty-four-year-old when I found out I was pregnant with my first baby. I was glowing with anticipation, and the colors surrounding me were as vibrant as my excitement. Months passed and fall arrived. As the air turned cool and the leaves blew from their high places down to the ground below, our lives changed forever. Instead of a blissful walk down the halls of labor and delivery, we walked a funeral procession to the room in the back corner. Our son was stillborn one month before his due date.

We were devastated when Owen died. Our whole world crashed down around us.

I'm now a mom of seven—four in my arms and three just out of sight. The grief over our missing children has not lessened in the years since we lost Owen. In fact, as the years go by and as the number of children in our arms outnumbers the children we have in heaven, it seems at times more confusing to share our grief and struggles.

In our church culture, I sense a powerful obligation to numb the hard in favor of something more positive, something that brings others more happiness and comfort than what hard can offer. I feel the tremendous pressure to gloss over the hard so we don't hurt our witness. And perhaps it's because we falsely believe that it shouldn't be so hard—if we just trust in Jesus, if we believe God is sovereign, if we place all our cares at His feet.

But what if hard is a part of the plan?

Hard can bring more hope than we ever thought possible. It will lead us to true hope when all our positive thinking runs out, when a time comes that we're not victorious over struggle and sin, when life keeps coming with brokenness after brokenness.

Hard will lead us to Jesus nailed to a cross.

As a bereaved mother who is also a pastor's wife, I have seen firsthand what can happen when we gloss over pain to point to the hope of heaven. When we do this, we actually highlight our own discomfort of hard, not the comfort of hope. We do not need to throw the blanket of God's sovereignty over the struggle and pretend that everything is okay. Life can be terribly hard *and* God can still be good.

I know it's difficult to enter into someone else's pain, but I've learned that we must be willing to be uncomfortable and bear the weight together if we're to show each other Christ.

One lonely day about six months after my son's death, a friend dropped by my apartment. She sat at my doorstep and gently knocked for about ten minutes. I would not, could not answer the door that day. Finally, she called and left a voicemail. "I'm here" came her voice on the message. "You don't have to answer the door, but I'm here." Her words acted like a tether to my aching heart. I felt seen, loved, and grounded from those two simple sentences. My friend chose to brave the uncomfortable, and in return I have carried her words as an Ebenezer stone of comfort.

In the midst of broken things, broken lives, broken bodies, broken relationships, we can stand firm in the hard and call out to others, *Come! God has not abandoned you. Come stand with us. Come lie down and rest. I can hold on for the both of us right now. Though the way is hard, our greatest hope is unchanging. Our hope is sure and lasting. Jesus is coming again, and nothing can separate us.*

PRAYER

Life is terribly hard, Lord, yet You are still good. Both at once. What a difficult, uncomfortable place to be. In the midst of these hard things, God, help me to stand firm in Your goodness. Help me cling to what is true: that You have not abandoned me, that my greatest hope is unchanging, that You are sure and lasting, and that I am unable to be separated from You. No matter what. In Your great name, amen.

Day 65

mestizo like Jesus

Foxes have dens and birds have nests, but the Son of Man has no place to lay his head.

Luke 9:58

I've always struggled to check the right box on forms. I am a brown-skinned Indian American woman with a bicultural identity. My father is of European descent, mostly German and British, and my mother is from India. When forced to choose a culture, my eyes go back and forth between the options "Caucasian" and "Asian," but neither feels quite right. I'm not white. I don't think, act, or even look like my white friends. We don't have the same histories. We have different values and even different food preferences. But I also don't consider myself to be Asian. That's not a term I hear Indians use. I also wasn't born in India. I understand Hindi better than I can speak it, and I don't wear Indian garb every day. So moments like this are a bit exhausting, often leading me down roads of identity confusion, where I'm not quite sure who I am or what I'm supposed to be.

I am a mestizo, a person in between worlds. I am no one and everyone, standing at the crossroads of so many different cultures, navigating other people's worlds, and struggling to find my place in it all. Equally complicated is the fact that others misunderstand and miscategorize me. My non-Indian friends often introduce me as "Michelle, the sort-of Indian." To my friends and relatives from India, I remain the "Americanized" woman who is not a true Indian. For now, having a bicultural identity means existing outside of cold categorizations and embracing the box of "other."

Thanks be to God, though, that I'm not the only one who's been a mestizo. Jesus was a mestizo long before me. In His incarnate form, He too had a bicultural identity. He was both God and man. He was a Jew growing up in first-century Palestine, and He spoke both His native tongue (Aramaic) and the language of the Roman Empire (Greek). Jesus knew, more than anyone, the feeling of being an outsider with no one to fully understand His personal experiences. He didn't fit in either. In Luke 9:58, He tells His disciples, "Foxes have dens and birds have nests, but the Son of Man has no place to lay his head." Jesus knew loneliness. He knew how it felt to be misunderstood and rejected.

That's why I keep my eyes on Christ. In Him, my identity belongs to something larger than me. Being a bicultural, Indian American woman makes me a mestizo like Jesus, and that's enough for me.

PRAYER

Jesus, I am so grateful that You get it. You understand the tension of being from two places. You have been in my shoes, and You have gone first, showing me that I am not alone in this struggle of being both-and, of not fitting in with the crowd. Thank You for also showing me how being different and an outsider makes me like You. Thank You for meeting me in this place. I am enough because You are enough for me. Amen.

Day 66

when worry is like
a rocking chair

Don't worry about anything; instead, pray about everything. Tell God what you need, and thank him for all he has done. Then you will experience God's peace, which exceeds anything we can understand. His peace will guard your hearts and minds as you live in Christ Jesus.

Philippians 4:6–7 NLT

Driving under a canopy of oak trees, I watched shadows dance with sunshine in the street. Their rhythm was slow and easy, calm and peaceful.

I felt the opposite. My tasks outnumbered my time, and worry outweighed my ability to focus and get things done. I was supposed to be at the library working on a project, but here I was driving around a pretty neighborhood, hoping these large southern-style homes with front porches and rocking chairs would give me the peace I longed for.

I pulled over and parked in the shade, leaned my head back on my seat, closed my eyes, and pictured myself in one of those rocking chairs. I took a deep breath and exhaled the pressure that had been building in my chest, and that's when a quote I'd read years ago came to mind: "Worry is like a rocking chair. It will give you something to do, but it won't get you anywhere!"

My worry was indeed like a rocking chair. Consuming concerns, distractions, and avoidance weren't getting me anywhere close to the peace I wanted or the progress I needed.

I pulled up my Bible app on my phone and read these words from the apostle Paul: "Don't worry about anything; instead, pray about everything. Tell God what you need and thank him for all he has done. Then you will experience God's peace, which exceeds anything we can understand. His peace will guard your hearts and minds as you live in Christ Jesus" (Phil. 4:6–7 NLT).

This was the wisdom I needed and the peace I'd been trying to find. I jotted down three things I could do to follow Paul's advice:

- Stop worrying—press the pause button on my consuming concerns.
- Start praying—open my mouth and tell God what I need.
- Keep thanking God—remind my heart of God's faithfulness by thanking Him for what He's already done in the past to help me trust what He will do in the present and future.

The next time worry takes you through the motions but doesn't get you anywhere, try Paul's way instead. It will take you through the motions of moving toward God. He is there, waiting to give you all you need.

PRAYER

Lord, thank You for the peace that comes when I put my trust in You! When worry threatens to take over my thoughts, help me remember to stop, talk to You, and thank You for what You've already done when I've been worried in the past. I need my heart to remember how good and capable You are of taking care of all that concerns me. Amen.

watch and wait

My soul waits for the Lord
more than watchmen for the morning,
more than watchmen for the morning.

Psalm 130:6 ESV

In the morning I wake up, stretch my arms up to the ceiling, and put on my glasses, watch, and a wedding band that sit on the nightstand. It's worth mentioning that my bed is a twin, I've never been married, and the ring was a hand-me-down from my mother when I was sixteen or so, right in the middle of the True Love Waits movement. For years I wore that ring on my left ring finger as a reminder of my commitment to wait for a spouse, but over time the purpose of the ring has changed.

It has become a reminder of the Lord's unfailing commitment to me, even on the days I can barely open my Bible. It represents companionship and doing life with a God who takes an interest in my day-to-day. This isn't some delusion of "Jesus is my boyfriend" spirituality. This is a ring that helps me see my relationship with Christ as one of marital-level commitment. Which makes sense, because it actually is.

"You know, you really need to take the ring off or men won't know you're single."

I started hearing that comment around the time I hit the age of desperation for so many—my mid-twenties. That's when it seemed like my fridge door was forever full of Save the Dates and Christmas cards from young couples and their goldendoodles. Like I had to change my strategy or men wouldn't know I was "available." As if once you got to know me for more than a few minutes, you wouldn't figure out I was unmarried.

And here's the hard question: why do we, in a culture of left-hand-ring-checking, use that info to decide whether someone is worth being friends with or talking to? It's just as unfair to befriend someone because they're single as it is because they're married.

As a single woman in the church, I'm used to these well-meaning ideas. I'm used to my friends and family wanting me to get married. But what happens when we turn into people who see one another for our marital status? What happens when we singles start to believe that we're just people in waiting? Psalm 130 reminds us that more than waiting for the right job or the right person or the right moment, we're all just waiting for Jesus—for His return and ultimately for the Marriage Supper of the Lamb. We are all bound for that marriage.

On this side of eternity, marriage is a good, holy thing. But it's not *the* good, holy thing.

As a single woman, I still wake up and put on that ring from time to time, and a dozen or so arguments plead their case for why that is or is not a good idea. But then I remember that even if my relationship status never changes, my Christ will always be near, and that will always be a commitment worth remembering and a relationship worth investing in. So we wait for Him with joy and hope, more than the watchman waits for the morning.

PRAYER

Lord, help me to wait well for the things I hope for, but more than that, help me to wait with expectancy for You and Your presence in my life. Amen.

Day 68

a resurrection of identity

I appeal to you therefore, brothers, by the mercies of God, to present your bodies as a living sacrifice, holy and acceptable to God, which is your spiritual worship. Do not be conformed to this world, but be transformed by the renewal of your mind, that by testing you may discern what is the will of God, what is good and acceptable and perfect.

Romans 12:1–2 ESV

My high school French teacher tried to convince our tired class why it was important to learn about the rest of the world and experience different cultures. I pretended I wasn't really listening and shoved the feeling that perked up inside me as far down as possible. She asked the class if anyone had ever lived in another country. I could feel my heart thumping. I didn't want to voice that I had lived in Japan and that my home was an amalgamation of Korean and European American culture.

I raised my hand a few inches, like my arm was half asleep. My teacher's eyes widened. She asked me to share. After I responded, she smiled and looked at me as if we had just made a deal. Like we had a silent understanding. She asked, "Doesn't it change everything?"

I knew it did, but I lied, "Not really." She looked away, deflated like a balloon, surrendered to a class of apathetic students.

For the longest time after becoming a Christian, I thought being in the world but not of the world only had to do with things like the kind of music I did or didn't listen to, the clothes I wore, and what I refused to consume. I had no idea that the Holy Spirit would seek to pry much deeper than those outward choices. With time, God began to slowly excavate the limited way I told my story and allowed myself to be seen.

I was convicted of the ways I had conformed to the world by assimilating parts of my Korean American identity. Cultural assimilation is an erasure, a hiding, a rejection, and a death. It's the process by which someone from a minority culture takes on the characteristics of the majority culture they are surrounded by, until their own unique cultural characteristics become invisible. But God pursued the hidden parts of my identity and showed me that He is the God of resurrection.

We have an enemy who works to kill, steal, and destroy. Assimilation works to kill specific God-formed parts of us. As the bride of Christ, all of us suffer because of this work. There's a pattern of pride and power that leads to hatred and oppression in the world. That pattern reinforces strongholds and systems of racism and tells stories that stem from false or incomplete narratives. The world would have all of us contribute and conform to these patterns. But those of us who follow Jesus are called to present our uniquely made bodies as living sacrifices, and to no longer conform to the patterns of our world but to be transformed by the renewing of our minds (Rom. 12:2). That means doing the work of living unassimilated lives and making space for those around us to do the same, day in and day out, is an act of everyday worship.

For me, it has meant grieving the years of hiding, pulling back layers of shame, leaning into the foods my Korean mom fed me, and remembering the stories she told me growing up. For the last ten years I've worked to learn how to embrace and live out my God-formed cultural identity while intentionally passing these things on to my kids. The grief of those hidden years never leaves, but now I have hope.

Jesus, our resurrected King, resurrects and renews the assimilated parts of our identity.

If I could go back in time, I would raise my hand high and tell my French teacher, "Yes, seeing and embracing these differences changes everything."

PRAYER

Lord, thank You for making me who I am, just as I am. I want to do the work of unassimilating so that the world can see the wonder and beauty of diversity that You created. Thank You for going first, for resurrecting and renewing the assimilated parts of my identity. I am so grateful. Amen.

Unity

was Jesus's vision for us,

and when it seems

like too much to even hope for it,

let's do as He did and

go to the Father.

Let's keep showing up

and asking in prayer

that we become

united in His love.

—LUCRETIA BERRY

Day 69

gaining ground when you feel defeated

The God of peace will soon crush Satan under your feet. The grace of our Lord Jesus be with you.

Romans 16:20

I sat at the shiny glass desk in the corner of my hotel room. I clicked back and forth between twelve open tabs. Checked my phone. Responded to another urgent email. Ignored the bing-bong of a text message. Over and over. And finally, I lost it.

I was at a large conference where I was slated to speak the next afternoon. Instead of a peaceful day soaking up encouragement from other presenters and connecting with friends, I was holed up in my hotel room solving problems I didn't create and putting out fires I didn't set. Compounded by weeks of relentless discouragement and distraction, it was more than I could take. I wept.

It wasn't just one thing. It's rarely ever just one thing.

My lungs heaved, trying to breathe under what felt like a lead blanket of opposition. At first the weight was bearable, but when it didn't lift, the oppression compounded. Normal breathing—normal thinking—felt impossible.

So there I was, with mascara running like muddy waterfalls down my face, no clear resolution to multiple issues in sight, and all the time to finish prepping my talk gone.

188

Where are You, God? I cried.

I collapsed onto the bed and wallowed in my own inadequacy to fix and control it all.

Then the voice of a friend interrupted my meltdown. Words spoken over me earlier in the week streamed into my thoughts like a fresh breeze on a stifling day. Stephanie had reminded me that when we're living out God's will for our lives, the enemy will do everything he can to thwart those plans. We can be distracted and disheartened by the attacks, or we can see them as confirmation of our effectiveness for the kingdom. Satan won't bother with something that's not a threat.

She also reminded me that, unlike God, Satan does not have access to our inner thoughts. So when we pray against the enemy in the power of Jesus's name, we have to pray out loud so he can hear us.

I had prayed all day for clarity. Really, I had been begging God for clarity for weeks. But now I did something different. I got up and prayed out loud.

With each word I vocalized, I grew in boldness and conviction. And I got angry. Really angry. Angry for every tear I had shed and all the stress I had internalized. For all the swirling anxiety and sleepless nights.

I stomped around that hotel room in my own *War Room*–like scene. I felt both ridiculous and empowered. I knew deep in my gut that I was in the thick of a battle I could not see.

Then, without forethought or intention, I heard myself say aloud, "Satan, you will gain no ground here!"

That was it. That was the crux of it all. God was in the business of gaining ground in women's hearts, and the enemy was after that same thing!

I lost it. Again. I sank to the floor and cried what felt like a year's worth of tears. Then . . . peace. Unlike anything I can explain.

This kind of thing doesn't happen to me every day. I know spiritual warfare is real because the Bible says so, but in my daily life I'm not thinking about combat in the spiritual realms.

But here's what I can't deny: one minute I was weighed down with discouragement, and the next I was uplifted with hope. One minute my heart and mind were in turmoil, the next I was enveloped with a peace that surpasses understanding.

Sometimes taking heart in the hard means taking into account the battles we *feel* but cannot see. We've got to start *seeing*.

PRAYER

Thank You, Lord, for the peace You give. The kind of peace that doesn't make sense. The kind of peace that doesn't belong. The kind of peace that causes fear to dissipate, turmoil to calm, ground to be gained. I can't explain this peace, except that it comes from You and You alone. God, bring that peace to my heart today. I'm in the thick of a battle unseen, and my only armor comes in and from You. Lead me, guide me, set my feet firmly, and help me to take heart—in peace. Amen.

Day 70

when you want to be the fixer

Give all your worries and cares to God, for he cares about you.

1 Peter 5:7 NLT

My closest girlfriends have nicknamed my therapist *Marg*, probably because I talk about her so much. I'm already an introspective woman, but it's amazing what a good therapist can cull out of you.

Sometimes I go in there and bawl my little cliché head off, but other times I go in there and we slap our knees. We laugh hard together. I tell her my funny stories, and it feels a lot like friendship, except I pay her and she can question my motives at every turn and bold-faced call me names like *martyr*. Once I considered breaking up with her as my therapist just so we could be actual friends, but wisdom told me better.

One time, Marg asked me about my friendships, about the role I play. I told her that as far back as I can remember I have been the friend to call in times of trouble. She was seeing a theme in my life. I had identified myself as a fixer, and in fact, there is not a time I can remember when I haven't loved that role. It's the thing I have to offer. I'm a burden bearer, the big sister, the secret keeper, and I love it.

The problem is, when *burden bearer* is the only name you call yourself, you begin to think the world will fall apart if you're not there to hold it together.

191

When my parents divorced several years ago, I found myself in one of the most painful seasons of my life. It opened my eyes even wider to see how many of us hurt in silence. Life keeps going. We lead in churches, fold all the clothes, run meetings, and buy groceries with a searing wound in our hearts. In times like these, it's interesting to see all the ways we hide and cope.

Somewhere along the way, I came to believe it was my sole purpose on earth to take on all the problems so those around me would be okay. I thought if I could hold it all together, maybe I'd be able to keep them from pain. But the truth was this: if I could deal with their pain, then maybe I wouldn't have to deal with mine.

The year my parents divorced, I broke. In fact, this was the kindest of mercies during that time. I was hurting and piling on the pain of others until I finally broke. I fell apart because I literally couldn't bear up under it anymore, and I realized I am not the fixer.

I had prayed for help to give my burdens and the burdens of others to God, but I never really believed until that year that He is the Fixer.

To believe that God is the Healer and the Burden Bearer brought more healing to my life than I had experienced in years. It's crazy how faith in His good character can do that.

Now I call my friends simply because they're my friends. Yes, sometimes they're hurting, but so am I. Other times we just laugh together. My capacity to share burdens is much greater now because I don't even pretend to hold up under pain. My friendships are more whole because things don't rest on me for long. I'm a better friend because I'm taking my own heart to the Healer instead of hiding it beneath other people's problems. I'm a better friend because I'm closer to laughter now than I've ever been.

I promise it's worth it to live like you're not the answer. I promise that a woman who withholds the burden from God is not the woman you should be calling in times of trouble. Call the woman who laughs. Be that woman.

Jesus, I am not the answer. May I immediately cease withholding the burden from You. I'm handing it over, Lord, relinquishing its weight to You, the only One who can bear it. May Your joy permeate the musty places that were occupied with the weight of burden, and may I be a woman who laughs. Amen.

suffering

Blessed are the poor in spirit,
for theirs is the kingdom of heaven.
Matthew 5:3

My mascara assures me its waterproof formula will hold strong, even when I can't make those same promises about myself.

I tell my story to the first psychiatrist to ask for it. Usually, doctors have my file open and are reading questions on a checklist, never looking up, never really seeing me. Sometimes they don't even bother to sit down. They wash their hands, scrubbing off their last patient, and then stand at the entrance to the exam room like they're halfway out the door before I've even said a word.

I'm a name scribbled on a prescription pad.

But this doctor settles into her chair like we're going to be here for a while. She looks like a woman accustomed to hearing people tell her their darkest thoughts and greatest fears. She listens when I tell her how the dark comes for me.

My eyes flick past her and up to a set of art drawings framed on the wall. They are marker-drawn animals, reminding me of my kids' art displayed with a magnet on the fridge. I need help because I want to live to see what else my kids create.

My sight settles on a rhino and the rest blur. I hope my mascara won't fail me. I dab at my eyes, holding a fistful of wadded-

194

up tissues clenched in my palm like I'm crushing all my emotions down to something manageable I can toss in the trash and leave behind on my way out.

I cannot imagine good could come of this. I worry my weakness disqualifies me.

I'm so exhausted from my depression that throwing on clean clothes and driving here leaves me wanting to curl up on her couch, curving my spine into a question mark while rocking myself into oblivion.

I come to Jesus begging, offering my anguish and fear and despair, my inability to fix myself. When the medications fail, when prayers seem unanswered, when Jesus seems silent, He's promised, "Blessed are the poor in spirit, for theirs is the kingdom of heaven." I am that—poor in spirit, lacking and desperate.

Weakness doesn't disqualify us. Even when we can't get out of bed, we're cherished and called by name.

Even when we think we have nothing to offer, Jesus is the blessing that meets us in our poverty. Maybe this is how the kingdom comes?

PRAYER

Lord, meet me in this place of weakness. I am poor in more ways than one, and You don't reject me. I tether myself to You and offer my empty hands for You to fill them and fill me. May Your kingdom come even in this place. Amen.

Day 72

God is our husband

For your Maker is your husband,
the Lord of hosts is his name;
and the Holy One of Israel is your Redeemer,
the God of the whole earth he is called.

Isaiah 54:5 ESV

We had stood in front of a picture window with a breathtaking mountain backdrop and snow dancing behind us. When we exchanged our vows on that afternoon, I meant every word I said. I never imagined twelve years later I would be living "till death do us part."

After my husband's battle with cancer and his death in 2014, I wasn't sure how to move forward without him. I began to realize my deepest grief came from no longer having my parenting partner and lover. Our daughters were ages two, five, and eight. They needed their mama to help them navigate grief.

Before I married Ericlee, I heard his grandmother share about Isaiah 54:5. She spoke passionately about how God is our husband and partner. These words carried me as a single girl, as a married woman when my husband was traveling, and eventually as a young widow.

This verse shifted my perspective about God and my situation. If God was my husband, I was no longer alone. In fact, I had the most perfect and dependable partner. When I was uncertain about a decision, when I needed strength to discipline my children, when I had to attend parent-teacher conferences or awards assemblies, when I was taking out the garbage and washing dishes, I clung to those words.

There was comfort in knowing that God, my Maker, also serves as my husband. He cares for me and partners with me. He imparts knowledge and courage to me when I call out for Him. He fills in what I lack. He transforms even the darkest circumstances for His glory.

As a solo parent and widow, I whispered quick prayers when I felt inadequate:

God, help me know what to do.

God, give me strength to train up this two-year-old.

God, show me how to help my girls through their grief.

He gifted me wisdom and creative parenting ideas I knew I didn't have on my own. He strengthened me to love my daughters even when I was exhausted from carrying the weight of providing for our family.

If you are a widow, a single mom, separated or divorced, a military wife, or even if your husband travels a lot, I want you to know you are not alone. The enemy of our souls would like us to feel isolated, downtrodden, and powerless, but the Lord Almighty is our husband. Who better to have on our team?

PRAYER

God, I love You, and I am deeply grateful that I don't have to be alone. You are with me. You are my husband, partner, helper, and friend. In my inadequacy, Lord, be enough. Help me know what to do. Show me how to help those I love with their grief. Give me strength and remind me that I'm truly not alone in this life but that You are always with me. Thank You, Lord. Amen.

Day 73

are we there yet?

Give thanks to the LORD, for he is good!
His faithful love endures forever.

Psalm 136:1 NLT

We thought we were pretty high-tech cruising down the road in our Pontiac Trans Sport minivan twenty-plus years ago. For long family road trips, we were among the first to have a "deluxe" videotape player that plugged into the cigarette lighter.

Cell phones and video games had not yet burst onto the scene, so when my kids invariably asked, "Are we there yet?" I would put it in terms they would understand: "One more *Winnie the Pooh* [thirty minutes] and we'll stop for something to eat." "One more *Sandlot* [ninety minutes] and we'll be there." This, along with a Mary Poppins bag of treats and toys that came out at crucial moments, is what got us through those long ventures.

As an adult who is cruising toward sixty, I find myself asking God, "Are we there yet?"

God has been so faithful to answer prayers in ways that I would have never imagined. Some prayers have gone on for over twenty-five years, and it's beginning to dawn on me that some prayers will not be answered on this side of eternity. We are drawn into thinking that this life is all there is and prayers need to be answered during this limited time we have on earth.

But God's promises go far beyond our short life spans. His focus is an eternal one, and He calls us to get on the bandwagon with this way of thinking. In a seminary class I took, one of the things they had us focus on in Scripture was repetition. When God really wants to make a point, the point is often repeated several times.

Psalm 136 chronicles God's steadfastness throughout biblical history, and after every point the psalmist makes, the chorus is repeated. "His faithful love endures forever" is repeated twenty-six times. I think God is trying to get the point across that His love is not just for this life but will be especially present in eternity—what hope, what joy awaits us!

The Bible talks a lot about *forever* and *eternity* and *life everlasting*. The gospel's main theme is that humanity is not doomed forever for our sins but by grace can have life everlasting, salvation in paradise forever.

I am convicted that I need to adjust my lens for a more eternal setting. This life is not all there is.

So when I want to ask God, "How long, O Lord?" it's kind of like I'm asking as a child, "Are we there yet?" As I try to patiently wait on the Lord, I take heart that even if my prayers aren't answered on this side of the pearly gates, they will certainly receive a glorious answer in eternity.

PRAYER

I thank You and praise You, God, that this life is not all there is. Thank You for sending Your Son to die for me so that I may live forever in eternity with You. Help me to be patient through these trials and periods of suffering, because I know they are building my character for eternal purposes. Help me to look not just to the end of this lifetime but to the blessing of eternal life, where all unanswered prayers will finally be answered once and for all. Grant me patience until I am with You forever. In Your eternal name, amen.

Day 74

hurt, hope, and making it through life's hard times

> Why am I discouraged?
> Why is my heart so sad?
> I will put my hope in God!
> I will praise him again—
> my Savior and my God!
>
> Psalm 42:5 NLT

The other day someone asked me about our infertility. It felt a bit like being asked about an old scar, one that has faded and become so familiar it feels more like a freckle. I paused for a long time, reaching back into those memories like one might rummage through a trunk in the attic.

I pulled out a single memory like a brightly colored scarf. One Christmas morning, we were visiting my in-laws and I felt certain I was pregnant. I jumped out of bed and practically skipped to the bathroom, only to be devastated again. My husband found me and put his arms around me, my tears soaking his T-shirt.

"Feel the hurt," I told this person. "It's real. Cry the tears. Yell into the pillow. Be sad and mad and confused."

Then I thought of another memory, a morning curled up under the covers, Bible in my hand. God took me to the third chapter of Genesis, where Eve is called the mother of all living things.

I began to understand that all women are mothers because all women bring life into the world in some way. I started to believe my story might be different than what I imagined—but it could still be good.

"Feel the hope," I said. "It's real. Embrace the unexpected. Trust that the story is still being written. Be curious and strong and brave."

You may not have walked through infertility, but if you're alive, then you know what it is to have trouble and heartbreak, to be disappointed, discouraged, or tired. I think in those moments we tend to choose one of the options above. We ignore everything but the hurt or everything but the hope.

We think that if we don't hope, then we can't be disappointed. Or that if we don't hurt, the pain can't overcome us.

But the reality is that hurt and hope are part of every hard experience. Hurt reveals our emotions so we can heal. Hope gives us the strength to persevere through that process. The wound slowly transforms. Then one day someone asks us about it and we're a bit startled because we realize what once felt like it might kill us has, in fact, taught us something about being fully alive.

We don't have to be afraid of hurt or afraid to hope. They are both part of what makes us who we are, part of our beauty and strength and scars.

PRAYER

Lord, infertility is a cruel thief, stealing joy from should-be-joyful moments and peace from could-be-extraordinary days. It makes hope seem too good to be true. What if I'm disappointed again? What about when the hurt comes and washes over me in waves? It's just easier not to hope, Lord. But I know that's not the kind of life You've called me to. I will put my hope in You. I will praise You again, Lord, even in the pain. I will call You good, and I will feel both the hurt and the hope. Amen.

Day 75

basic questions on the playground of life

When I am afraid, I put my trust in you.
Psalm 56:3

I have a son who is autistic. He is just past the category of nonverbal into a sort of pre-conversation. He can sound out words, repeat them, and at times use them intentionally but in a scripted way. If an average six-year-old has approximately 2,600 expressive words and 20,000 to 24,000 receptive words in their vocabulary, you can imagine my eight-year-old has far less at his disposal. Only the Lord knows the fullness and depth of him.

All our efforts toward behavioral, speech, and occupational therapy did not yield as much headway for conversation as my husband and I had dreamed of. For someone like me who loves connection, conversation seemed key, but that key was lost somewhere, and we've been flipping our lives upside down trying to recover it.

We want our son to be able to answer basic questions, if not as a building block for relationships, then at least for safety reasons.

"What's your name? How old are you? What's your mom's phone number?" we drill into him. "What school do you go to? What's your address?" we ask, knowing full well that any change in life, such as a future move of school or home, would wash away all our efforts and bring us back to square one.

If I'm honest, the intensity of our efforts reveals our forethought and wise anticipation as much as our secret, beastly anxieties. *What's your name? Do you know your name? Will that be enough to keep you safe?*

In response to my endless demands to secure that elusive peace, my son looked at me one day and paused. "What's your name?" I asked again. He didn't answer. His eyes wandered to the playground.

Oh no, honey, give me eyes—look me in the eyes. What's your name?

As the beast of anxiety began to wrap its intimidating claws around me, I saw my son's eyes brighten and glimmer to flash a mischievous little boy I had long forgotten.

In a cheery voice, my son replied with an ear-to-ear smile, "I'm slide!"

Confused, I asked, "You're . . . what?"

"I'm slide!" he said, not just with his words but also with his twinkling, staying eyes.

He looked at the slide and then back at me, as if for me to track with him—*Do you see what I see, Mom? Come on, join me! I already know my name. Instead, I'm going to surprise you by saying I am the first fun thing I see. I'm trying to get you to lighten up! Take off your anxieties and see what I'm doing!*

"I'm slide!"

My son had made his first joke.

Faith rose up in me as I realized my son was leading me out of the stiff and stuffy quasi-conversation into something new and fresh—something like a breakthrough. He had found a delightful escape from my incessant drills by turning it on its head and making a joke. By that simple, creative use of seemingly unrelated—even wrong—things, my son made a way where there seemed to be no way, inviting me into the genuine connection that my heart longed for.

My son's lean vocabulary has since only added delight and gratitude whenever I happen upon—am gifted with—his witty, charming, wonderful self. Autism still dots our lives with a chaotic, confusing, frenzied scattering of dots, but I look now with eyes of faith, searching for signs of grace. I am looking for Jesus in all the surprising ways that He may show up on the playground of life, because He's already with us, beckoning our notice. So now my basic questions have changed. They are still building blocks for relationship and safety, but now they're insistently aimed toward Jesus: "Jesus, where are You? What are You doing?"

PRAYER

God, sometimes I am so overcome with anxiety and fear that I don't realize how it has taken hold of me until I see how tense I have become toward others and myself. Instead of trying to control my life, I want to become aware of Your active presence in my life. Give me ears to hear and eyes to see. Amen.

Day 76

do you have an exit strategy?

Train up a child in the way he should go: and when he is old, he will not depart from it.

Proverbs 22:6 KJV

As my children get older, I try to imagine what our empty nest years will look like. Our family of ten has lived loud and large for a long time, so it's hard to imagine a quiet, almost-empty house. Watching children move out and transition to their adult lives requires a period of adjustment for any mom. It's easy to wrap our identity in roles that have a time limit: homeroom mother, soccer mom, homeschool teacher, softball coach, PTA president. How will we occupy our days when our years have been filled with cross-country meets, baseball games, dance recitals, and gymnastics lessons?

I used to think I'd be obsolete by the time our last child leaves home, that whatever I could offer the world would be hopelessly dated. But then I realized it would not only benefit me but also my children if I didn't wait until they left to pursue some interests of my own.

So I started a blog and a web design business. Then I bought a camera and studied photography and Photoshop. I taught myself the skills I needed using books and the internet. Now I teach about healthy living and essential oils, strengthening friendships, and creating more ways to stay connected with my circle of mom friends after my children graduate.

I've learned there's always something new that I can learn, even if I've never done it before. And even though I'm approaching a time when the house will be quieter, with fewer kids needing me, it doesn't mean that I don't have people and places I can still pour into.

What about you? Are there dreams you never pursued? Did you love to paint? Sew? Write? Do you want to take or teach classes? It's not too late to make plans so that when your nest is empty, your days may be full.

And look around you. Perhaps there are others you can build new friendships with—people in seasons ahead of you and behind you in whom you can invest your time and care. You're exiting one season but entering a new one, so in the transition pay attention to the things that pull at your heart, to the areas of your life that may need more care, and don't be afraid to start planning and dreaming.

PRAYER

Lord, I've trained my children up, and soon they'll have flown the coop. I will be in a whole new place, in a whole new way, and I need You to guide me there. I don't want to be unsure of what to do or even of who I am, so help me start investing now. I want my kids to see me living my own life, my own dreams, and so I will follow Your lead, Lord. Help me exit well. Amen.

Day 77

discovering beauty amidst busyness

He has made everything beautiful in its time.

Ecclesiastes 3:11

Have you ever been so busy that you felt like you could barely keep your head above water? I remember one fall when the school year had just begun, my corporate job was particularly intense, and life was just overwhelming in every aspect.

I realized that I needed to slow down. I needed to breathe. I needed a change. And while most of my work deadlines couldn't be changed, my perspective could. I was too hurried to take in the beauty around me.

It started out organically. I saw a blooming tree and snapped a picture of it. Then I saw the most incredible sunset, and I just stopped, watching the clouds roll by. My daughter played happily in the lake, and I took a photo, wanting to never forget her joy.

Over time, discovering everyday beauty became a daily adventure. In the morning I'd think, *What will I discover today? Where is the beauty?* The answer: everywhere.

Beauty in nature. Beauty in people. Beauty in vulnerability. Beauty in the mess of every day.

Sometimes I take out my phone and snap a picture, wanting a tangible reminder of what I found that day. Other days I simply acknowledge the beauty and continue about my day. The act of acknowledgment is powerful and life-changing.

It's all a wonder. It's all a gift. Taking the time to soak in the ordinary wonderful has been an important reminder to me that life is meant to be savored.

While work and deadlines are important, they don't need to be soul-draining. They too can be life-giving if my perspective is one of beauty.

The beauty in the world.

The beauty in the opportunities.

The beauty in the growth that happens because of the work.

Scripture says that God has made everything beautiful. Seeing life through that lens is profound and life-giving.

May we appreciate the beauty this world has to offer, even if our circumstances are busy, stressful, or sad. And as we take it in, may our lives overflow with beauty to those around us.

PRAYER

God, I need to slow down. I can feel the drain on my soul, and I want to stop it before it runs dry. Give me eyes to see the everyday beauty happening all around me, all the time. Shift my perspective and help me see all that You have made beautiful. Amen.

if life doesn't look like what you hoped for

We know that all things work together for the good of those who love God, who are called according to his purpose.

Romans 8:28 CSB

Sitting at the table on Thanksgiving, turkey sandwich in front of me and empty seats all around, this thought unexpectedly crossed my mind: *you are lacking no good thing.*

It caught me by surprise, seemingly out of place in the middle of a season of grief, loss, and changes that were both unexpected and unwanted.

Wiping crumbs from the table and turning the phrase over in my head, I quietly offered these words in response: "I believe You, God, but right now I feel lonely, I see lack, and I hear silence. Help me look past what isn't to what is, and help me call it good."

Reaching for a piece of paper, I began to intentionally write down the gifts God had lavishly poured out: Relationships seemingly broken beyond repair now mended back together. Four surgeries before age twenty-six, all with the same result: benign. His financial provision through years of ups and downs.

Looking at the list, I realized each gift came from a storm I wouldn't have chosen. Over time, the very waves that threatened to take me out pushed me to shore. The flames that threatened to destroy became the fire that refined. And when everything around was shaking, God was a solid foundation.

God was there in all of it—in the hard and the holy. In the ordinary, He was waiting to be found. In the unknown, He was constant. In the broken places, He was holding me together.

The truth was clear: God redeems every last thing. He is a way-making, promise-keeping, battle-winning, water-walking, storm-stilling, faithful Friend and Savior.

My list of what isn't didn't change after making my list of what is—but my perspective did.

Maybe there are gifts hidden in the timing of the answer and in the prayers that seemingly receive a no.

This isn't what I expected my right-now life to look like, but I trust the Author. I have to believe this is exactly what I would choose for myself if I could see the entire storyline.

He is a good God, a loving Father who gives good gifts to His children—gifts of what is and what isn't. And so today, here with my two lists, I will choose to be grateful in the hard and in the holy, trusting He is with me in both.

PRAYER

God, I want to believe You when You say I lack no good thing. Help me to remember the ways You have been faithful. Help me to look past what isn't to what is and to call it good. I know You're waiting to be found. Give me eyes to seek You and strength to find You in both hard and holy moments. Amen.

I am broken.

I am needy.

I can't fix myself.

That's where I see the

incredible beauty
of God's grace.

There is hope in that broken

and needy place.

—LISA LEONARD

what going to the dentist taught me about self-care

So the heavens and the earth and everything in them were completed. On the seventh day God had completed his work that he had done, and he rested on the seventh day from all his work that he had done. God blessed the seventh day and declared it holy, for on it he rested from all his work of creation.

Genesis 2:1–3 CSB

Last year I went to the dentist more than a dozen times.

Yes, that is many more dental appointments than the standard two cleanings a year. See, for years my teeth were neglected as my body grew three babies and made their food from scratch. My three babies took all my calcium and tooth-enamel-building vitamins for themselves while they were growing and nursing, and *poof*, my teeth were ruined.

Also, I'm pretty skittish about the dentist and require a light level of sedation to get in the chair, which wasn't possible during pregnancy. So I didn't go for a cleaning or exam until I started bringing my kids to the dentist. I figured if they went, I should too, so I scheduled my first visit in four years. After scrubbing my poor teeth, the dentist gently said, "Let's get your next cleaning on the calendar before you leave today, okay?" We also booked a consult to create a long-term plan for fixing my damaged teeth. I'm now more than halfway through that plan . . . and have yet to shake the shame.

Thoughts of shame roll through my head. *How could I have let this get so bad? How could I take such intentional care of my kids and not of my own self? Why do I have to be so scared of this? No one else has this issue! This is dumb. I am dumb. I'm costing us so much money as we fix this mess!* What began in fear grew into a mountain of despair so unapproachable that I hid from it for years, and the shame built up.

One week, after trudging to an appointment, I messaged a friend from the parking lot. I told her about how ashamed I was feeling, how embarrassed I was by the product of my own neglect and fear. My friend replied right away that due to a situation of her own, she understood my feelings. And then she said that despite the embarrassment and shame rolling around my heart, I could be proud of myself because I was doing the work. I was making (and keeping) all my appointments. I was doing the hard work of repair, and I could be proud of the future I was working toward instead of being swallowed up by the shame of what got me here.

Naturally I teared up, and then I started to shed the shame spiral, because there is no shame in taking care of myself.

Going to the dentist is self-care. Taking a walk is self-care. Taking care of yourself *is* self-care. It's not pedicures and lattes. Those things are great (make mine a double, with skim milk and one pump of hazelnut, please), but they aren't lasting, intentional care. Going to the dentist isn't fun, but it means taking deeper care of myself than just drinking a latte.

Real self-care, the kind that actually takes *care* of one's *self*, is scriptural.

In the beginning of Genesis, God created the heavens and the earth and everything in it, but at the end of it all, He also created Sabbath, showing us that rest is an essential part of how we are to live. It wasn't meant to be a luxury but a necessity.

So there's no shame in taking care of yourself, be it resting or going to the dentist. We never have to be too ashamed to start good, healthy, care-filled habits. Make the appointment you've been putting off. Drop the shame. Take care of yourself. You can do this.

PRAYER

God, in caring for others, I put myself and my needs aside, going from one thing to the next without stopping to rest. You, who are all-powerful and all-knowing, rested after the work of creation, so help me to learn from You. Teach me to care for myself—love myself—as You love me.

Day 80

when your child chooses a different way

Trust in the LORD with all your heart;
    do not depend on your own understanding.
Seek his will in all you do,
    and he will show you which path to take.

Proverbs 3:5–6 NLT

Sometimes our children choose a path that seems to wind and twist and loop back on itself. Sometimes it seems they prefer to walk right along the edge of the cliff, where the limestone crumbles away beneath their feet with every step they take. They teeter on the precipice—their arms outstretched, refusing to heed our calls to come back from the edge or to take a different path or to choose the road we highlighted for them on the map.

Our heart beats fast, and our hair turns gray, and we wring our hands as we watch them tempt fate. They laugh at us or wave us off, or maybe they don't even turn to look in our direction. We toss and turn at night and then fall asleep at stoplights in broad daylight.

We write laments in journals. We submit prayer requests, and we sign them "Anonymous" because the story doesn't just belong to us. We pray and give up praying. We cry and shout and whisper and grow silent, and our heart sits heavy in our chest. We hold our breath.

I'm only telling my own story here. I'm offering it up in case there is another someone out there who has tried everything she can to fix it or to make it right or to call her child back from the edge. I just want to tell you that you are not alone.

And I want to tell you, God's got this. He does. So go ahead and breathe.

I don't say that lightly. It's hard to breathe when every phone call makes your lungs stop cold. And if you remember to breathe today, by tomorrow you might forget again.

One day I sat breathless before God. My gut was twisted in a knot, and I couldn't even look in His direction. My hands fell open in my lap, and I whispered, "What am I supposed to do?" And just as quickly as I asked the question, one word slipped its way into my heart: "Love."

I can do that, I thought. *I can love. But what else, God?*

"Just love," He breathed into my heart. "I'll do the rest. I've got this. All you have to do is love."

PRAYER

God, Your way is love. Sometimes it seems too simple to be effective and too good to be true, but that is what changed my heart toward You. Help me to do the same for my child(ren). Help me to love in that far-reaching way You love me. I entrust my child(ren) to You. Amen.

Day 81

God will give you strength

Fear not, for I am with you;
   be not dismayed, for I am your God;
I will strengthen you, I will help you,
   I will uphold you with my righteous right hand.

Isaiah 41:10 ESV

Several years ago my brother-in-law was killed in a motorcycle accident. Obviously, no time is a good one for the unexpected death of a family member, but this really seemed to come at the worst possible time in my life. See, I was already entrenched in two intense battles, one for my marriage and one with my four-year-old daughter.

Standing in that hospital waiting room, the news felt unbearable. It was surely more than we could stand! I just knew it would be the final blow for our little family, for my husband's faith, for my own heart.

In hindsight I know the news was, in fact, unbearable. For my husband's family, who had already experienced great tragedy and loss. For my little girl, who adored her uncle and didn't quite understand the concepts of death and forever and heaven. But for my husband and me, who were barely speaking, what we faced was absolutely excruciating.

We could not possibly stand on our own, much less fight our way through grief and logistics, emotions and questions, too much time together and not enough time left. If we'd had only our own strength to draw from in that season, we would have buckled for sure.

And certainly we had moments, days, weeks when we did just that. But never for too long and never permanently. Instead, we were able to reach for the supernatural strength God offers us—the strength to stand under the weight of sorrow, to turn toward each other rather than toward comfort found elsewhere, to take one step, then another and another and another.

Some of those steps were physical—making funeral plans, making a slideshow of photos, and asking questions about insurance, custody, and organ donation. Some of those steps were emotional—reaching out to friends for counsel and comfort when we would have rather hidden and wallowed, ignoring slights and irritations borne out of too little sleep, responding gently to thoughtless words spoken in grief. Honestly, just holding my tongue as I spent days on end with my devastated in-laws took determination and wisdom I do not normally possess.

Everything we did and said and didn't say and didn't do in the days and weeks that followed that crisis was an exercise requiring strength I would not have imagined we had. But by turning to God and leaning on Him, we were able to tap into everything He has and offers us. We were able to make it through what felt like the darkest timeline. We were able to withstand the fire that for a while seemed unending and make it to the other side of the battleground.

What kind of battle are you in today? Who is coming after your spirit, your stability, your livelihood, your loved ones? What is attacking your health, your resilience, your perseverance, your faith?

Death is a harsh reality, but it's far from the only hard thing we face. Divorce, disease, job loss, the death of a dream. Infertility, insecurity, anxiety, boredom. Temptation, addiction, unfair treatment, silence, or isolation. It seems like this world is constantly looking for new ways to cause us pain, and maybe it is.

No matter what kind of trouble you are facing in your life, God will give you the strength to endure. Some seasons and situations are truly unbearable. But when you cannot stand on your own, when your faith and strength fail you, God will be right there to prop you up and propel you forward. He promises to help us and to hold us, and He will.

PRAYER

When it rains, it pours, and right now, Lord, I'm soaking wet. This struggle I'm facing only seems to be getting bigger, and other battles are joining in. I am struggling to stay above water. Lord, give me the strength to endure. Prop me up and propel me forward. I need You to help me and hold me and see me through all the way to the other side of this fight. Amen.

Day 82

when all that remains is only Jesus

I am the vine; you are the branches. If you remain in me and I in you, you will bear much fruit; apart from me you can do nothing.

John 15:5

I left my work in church ministry several years ago, and since then I've been asking God for a new vision for my life. I grew up hearing the King James Version of Proverbs 29:18 said with almost folkloric caution: "Where there is no vision, the people perish." It was laced with passion, purpose, and warning. *Don't be without vision, or you* will *perish*, it seemed to say.

But every time I've asked, it seemed as though God's voice would get lost in the fog. No matter how much I strained to hear with my soul, it was as though I wasn't listening well enough to catch His quiet whisper. I questioned myself, my motives, my faith, but even then I would come up empty. Nothing seemed to be wrong, and God's presence was still near and His voice in other matters was clear.

I began to wonder what it meant if God never gave me another vision. Could I still live a meaningful, purposeful life for His kingdom? What does it mean to have a calling when there is no vision for it?

And in the midst of my questioning, as I cried out again in restlessness, I felt God say to me that He was covering my eyes, keeping me from seeing the vision, and that was a grace to me. He assured me that I was right where I was supposed to be, and then it seemed to make sense: I may not have a vision for my life or even for this season, but if all that remains is only Jesus, there is still purpose to my life. I can still bear much fruit. I am not detached from Him but must continue to remain in Him.

When all the striving, all the gifts, all the callings and passions are set aside, and when all that remains is only Jesus, take heart. You're not lost. You're not without purpose. Stay near and abide in Christ, and that is enough.

PRAYER

Lord, at the very core of what You have called us to do is the invitation and command to abide. Even in that, we need help. So when we get restless in the mundane rhythms of life, center us, ground us to Jesus, Your Son, who is our everything and the reason for everything. Amen.

Day 83

you are worth taking care of

Come to me, all you who are weary and burdened, and I will give you rest.

Matthew 11:28

She was standing in front of the flower bouquets at Trader Joe's, unsure of herself.

"What are you deciding between?" I turned to ask, smiling.

She let me know she was having a hard time deciding and often would go home without flowers because she couldn't choose.

"Me too," I said. "I couldn't decide between flowers I really wanted and ones that cost less."

"Exactly!" she agreed.

"I'd talk myself out of it," I confided. "I'd think to myself, *It's not worth it. They'll only last a few days.* What I later realized was that I was actually saying, *I'm not worth it. What I find joy in for just a few days isn't worth it.*"

"So true." She nodded. When I asked what flowers she loved as a little girl, she shared about how sunflowers reminded her of summer and riding her bike with a basket adorned with a plastic sunflower.

"There's something about flowers," I said. "Something about how God made them. I read that scientific studies show simply looking at flowers improves emotional health."

I told her I'd lost my spark a few years earlier and needed to learn to take better care of my well-being. Women are heroes when it comes to loving and caring for others, but why is it so hard to give ourselves permission to rest and refresh when we're stressed and need it most?

I gently placed my hand on her shoulder and affirmed to her, "You're worth it. You are worth taking care of."

Deep inside us, God created an inner spirit that needs nurturing. We're made to be loved, cared for, and given attention. We all need permission to take better care of ourselves. We all need a friend to help us remember we are like beautiful flowers blossoming in the fields.

God doesn't want us to do more for Him. He longs to take care of us and whisper words of love and peace. Instead of layering on guilt when you feel stressed, let God love you and care for you. Choose to rest. Choose to enjoy the beauty He's given around you. And don't hesitate to get yourself some flowers.

PRAYER

Today, Lord, I am going to get the flowers. Maybe not actual blooms, but whatever it is that gives me joy. Thank You for reminding me that I am worth it because You created me with worth. Nurture me when I lose grace for myself. Help me to learn how to rest and receive Your loving care. I want to see more of You in the beauty all around me. I love You, Lord. Amen.

Day 84

God is good, but this isn't

Yet I am confident I will see the LORD's goodness
while I am here in the land of the living.

Psalm 27:13 NLT

Seven hundred women sing with reckless abandon, "You are good, good, oh. You are good, good, oh." Hands stretch high as they harmonize the heavenly tune. I try to sing with them, but something in my spiritual gut cracks open. The well deep inside bursts, and I double over in a silent scream.

God is good, but this isn't.

Piercing pain and loss beyond words rupture my soul. My precious friend is gone. We prayed every single day for over a year, claiming healing Scriptures over her body, fasting, pleading, proclaiming, declaring. I believed. She believed. So many people believed that the miracle would come.

But she is now with the Lord, rejoicing. Her husband and five children are here, grieving.

I don't understand why Scripture says one thing when sometimes reality seems to say another. There must be a loftier view. There must be a greater truth. Higher ways. Higher thoughts. I know the verse, but it offers little comfort to me now. What is this way that is so much higher than mine? What are these higher thoughts of the Divine?

I know that Scripture is faith, not formula, but that where two or more are gathered in Christ's name, He is there. He has given us authority. We can command mountains, like cancer, to be removed and cast into the sea. We did, but cancer remained. Cancer took my friend home and left her family here.

I know that God didn't cause this, but He could've answered differently. Sometimes I long to be God so that I can tell a different story. Yes, the story would've turned out differently if *I* had written it. It would've been miraculous and triumphant and victorious!

But the second such thoughts take hold, I know that I am far too small and unqualified to write my own story, much less anyone else's. After all, if I had written Jesus's story, He wouldn't have died either.

The song continues. *You are good, good, oh.*

Sometimes you have to make a choice. You can wait for the song to change, or you can let the song change you. That's when a song can become more than a song.

A song can become an act of war, a prophetic proclamation, an emphatic declaration that what I see today will not be what I see tomorrow. A song can become a testimony confirming that the story *is* miraculous and triumphant and victorious, but we haven't gotten to that part of the story yet.

Sometimes we must sing what we *believe*, not what we *feel*. We must sing what we *know*, not what we *see*.

So I sing—not as a reflection of this present reality but as a declaration of who God is despite this present reality.

I sing in gratefulness that my friend's suffering is over. I sing in humble faith that the suffering her family must now endure will not be without redemption. I sing, commanding the bad that is right now to surrender to the good that is to come. I sing not because of what I see today but because of what I *have* seen and what I *will* see again—the goodness of my God in the land of the living (Ps. 27:13).

"You are good, good, oh. You are good, good, oh."

God, even in this, I will sing. I want to see Your goodness here. I am looking to see Your goodness even in this circumstance. Lord, help me sing when my heart is breaking. Help me sing what I actually believe, not what I feel or even what I see, because I know what is visible to me isn't the whole story. In Your holy name, amen.

trusting God
when life is messy

And Mary said, "Behold, I am the servant of the Lord; let it be to me according to your word." And the angel departed from her.

Luke 1:38 ESV

I feel like I'm almost always in "one of those seasons"—the difficult season that seems so messy and frustrating and long. The one that fills me with doubt, worry, and questions. My husband not completely healing. My health issues. Trying to run an art business. My loved ones struggling in a variety of ways.

It's hard to believe God has an almighty plan through all this mess. Things seem so broken. I wonder if there is an end to all the madness.

Just how is He working through all these issues and struggles? If only we had the answers, if we knew what was going to happen next, wouldn't it make it easier to trust God's plan? If we were given full disclosure of God's plan in our lives, wouldn't we be at complete peace?

I'm guessing if we were actually shown God's plan, many of us, including me, would probably think it doesn't make sense, and we would just have more questions.

227

We like to be in control. We think we need to be in control. Trust takes that sense of control away and gives it to someone else.

Mary's response to the angel is a beautiful example of that kind of trust. Her focus wasn't inward. She didn't ask how this would change her life. She didn't ask dozens of questions. Her response was simple. She surrendered to God's will. She trusted if that was God's plan for her, it must be good.

From our point of view, things can look messy, but that isn't the view that matters most. God has the correct point of view. He has worked through the messy before, so we know we can trust He will continue to work through it.

Remember, God doesn't want us to live with doubt and fear weighing so heavily on us. He wants us to live in peace and security, trusting Him and His ways.

So don't worry about what's next—God is next. God is our steady. That is the beauty of a life tuned to His truth.

I do not know where He is directing me in this season, but I am trusting my walk with Him. I am trusting there is meaning and purpose in each season. And I am just going to let it be.

PRAYER

In this particular season, it seems that everything is an unresolved mess, God. I can't see past the struggle, and it's weighing so heavily on my heart. I need You to pick it up. I need a portion of Mary's faith, the kind that trusts You wholeheartedly even when nothing makes sense. Today, Lord, I want to experience Your presence, the steadiness You offer when I'm on shaky ground, and the view from Your vantage point instead of mine. I want to live attuned to Your truth. Amen.

Doubt doesn't mean disbelief.

The questions can lead us to God's presence.

Our doubt can deepen
our intimacy.

—TASHA JUN

Day 86

surrendering to the God who sees

I am weary with my moaning;
every night I flood my bed with tears;
I drench my couch with my weeping.

Psalm 6:6 ESV

I was ten hours from home, on vacation with my oldest daughter and her children, when I received the shocking call from my husband. My son had died; he had taken his own life.

Never would we have imagined such devastating loss.

Suicide was a word *other* people discussed, cried over, and otherwise grappled with. It was never a word I *needed* to consider. My life had the picket fence, the green grass, and the stuff dreams are made of.

Until that day five years ago, when the world I knew crumbled at my feet.

Initially, I was in shock. Then the busyness of the funeral preparations left me with no time to feel. Eventually, after life went back to normal for everyone else, I found myself in a dark, lonely place—feeling split wide open and spilled out, terrified I'd be there forever. The unanswerable question of *why* pierced every thought and crushed my soul.

Where was God when my son took his life? Where was He when all I wanted to do in my grieving was go to sleep and never wake up? Where was He when my family was grief-stricken to the point of despair?

I needed the comfort of knowing God was there holding me, but I couldn't bring myself to talk to Him. I was angry and confused. I had nothing to say to Him.

Finally, after weeks of struggling to find a sliver of hope, I gathered enough nerve to ask God what He was thinking.

When are You planning to help me? How long will I cry and toss around in my bed without finding sleep? How long will You leave me here—alone?

Wearily, and even reluctantly, I reached for the Bible I hadn't been able to open since my son died and opened it to the Psalms. There I found words of sorrow and anguish so much like my own:

> I am weary with my moaning;
>   every night I flood my bed with tears;
>   I drench my couch with my weeping. (Ps. 6:6 ESV)

As I dug deeper into the Psalms, I discovered that David, the shepherd boy, psalmist, and eventual king of Israel, also faced grief and suffering. After reading his words in this psalm and others, my heart understood what David discovered long ago: God wants to hear from His children. He can handle our questions and our anger. He allows us to lament.

Lament—pouring it out to God unreservedly—is biblical and is truly a gift for the hurting heart. When we are overwrought with grief and drowning in a sea of questions, lament is an invitation to give our pain and our questions to the God who sees, who is big enough to handle it all.

My heart is broken over the loss of my son, and grief will be with me until I'm standing in the presence of Jesus. But pouring out my heart to God allows me to experience hope while I am still in the suffering.

PRAYER

God, I am full of lament. My heart is shattered, my world drowning in grief. Thank You for meeting me in this place of despair, of loss. You understand what it's like to lose Your Son. Please sit with me as I grieve. Amen.

Day 87

when shame wakes you up at three in the morning

So if the Son sets you free, you are free through and through.

John 8:36 MSG

Shame woke me up at three in the morning. My eyes flew open, and I felt as though I hadn't yet slept. Suddenly I was wide awake and acutely aware of the shame wrapped around me.

It was late, and I felt like the smallest human on earth. I made my way into the fetal position, my white bedspread crumpled beside me, a tangible example of how I felt within.

"I don't understand," I whispered to Jesus. "I have dealt with my insecurities. I have come to terms that I am enough as I am. Why do I feel so small? So worthless?"

My shame thrives at three in the morning, when the wind is banging my blinds against the wall, when the darkness is at its darkest. Like a boa constrictor, shame snakes around me, squeezing. Soon I am poured out and exhausted.

I closed my eyes and took a deep, clear breath, silently begging Jesus to unravel me from the tangled mess I found myself in. I asked myself, *What is my feeling, and what is my truth?*

There's a difference, I know. My feelings don't dictate what is true. It's just harder to remember that when I'm in the midst of feeling things strongly.

233

My feeling: I am not enough.

My truth: I am. I am. I am.

My feeling: I will always live in a prison of shame.

My truth: Jesus has set me free—and who the Son sets free is free indeed.

My feeling: What I produce is not meaningful.

My truth: My life is meaningful and sacred and significant, and because my work stems from my life, my work is important too.

Shame does not decide who I am, although that's trickier to declare when my heart is weary and shame has a good, strong grasp.

Shame woke me up at three in the morning, and then my alarm woke me up at seven. I looked at my room, now bathed in light instead of the darkness I saw earlier. I gathered my truths instead of my feelings and held them close against me for the rest of the day.

And I said, "Jesus, teach me what is true, teach me what is true, teach me what is true."

Because even when I don't feel enough, I'll hold on like a mad woman to the truth that I am.

PRAYER

Take my shame, God. Release me from the lies that reverberate in my head and heart; replace them with Your truth and lead me into the light of day. Jesus, teach me what is true, over and over again. Help me hang on to Your promises and Your peace. Amen.

Day 88

faith is made for miracles

Now faith is confidence in what we hope for and assurance about what we do not see.

Hebrews 11:1

I had only just met her, and for some reason I felt the Holy Spirit prompting me to encourage my new acquaintance that she would indeed give birth to a baby. It seemed wrong and against every rule to say that to someone who was in the midst of infertility woes, and I had no idea why I was being recruited to be in proximity to her pain. I didn't even know her well, but what I did know was that I had seen a vision of her full-term pregnancy and that I was to pray for and cheer her on until the baby arrived.

She said it would take a miracle for them to conceive, and that's when things started to make more sense. A miracle was God's plan all along, but praying and waiting for a miracle to happen felt weighty and overwhelming. I felt too small for the task, and I was intimidated. In that moment of feeling inadequate to be part of something so big, I experienced faith differently than I had before. Faith is designed to go where we've yet to go and hold space until we arrive.

As a monument of faith, I set aside my cherished basket bassinet, the one our babies had slept in nestled next to my bedside. To faithfully pray and cheer, I needed to hold space for the victory, and I knew I would one day gift the bassinet

235

to the new mom. So when the time came to give away all our past-the-baby-stage stuff, we kept the bassinet. When we moved to another city, the bassinet moved with us, as a sign for us to keep praying, to have faith, and to hold space for the miracle.

And when the couple conceived, the doctors recognized it for what it was—truly a miracle! What a privilege it was to walk alongside them!

Faith is a reality that can be trusted. In faith, we can say yes (even reluctantly) to God's most awkward and faith-stretching requests, knowing that ultimately a masterpiece will manifest and we will get to witness miracles.

PRAYER

God, give me the faith to trust in You and to believe in the reality of what I cannot see. Help me hold on to that hope for others when they need it. Amen.

when marriage isn't a hallmark movie

Whoever wants to be my disciple must deny themselves and take up their cross daily and follow me. For whoever wants to save their life will lose it, but whoever loses their life for me will save it.

Luke 9:23-24

I watched them walking down the sidewalk, hands intertwined, faces filled with happiness. Husband and wife, they moved in comfortable tandem, without urgency or anxiety. They looked like something plucked from the pages of a romance novel—young, attractive, and very much in love.

Then I took stock of my current relationship scenario. I, too, was married, but for a second time, after divorce had ripped the fairy tale out of my hands. Rather than unending romance, our marriage came with the challenges of a blended family—both biological children and stepchildren. Then, ten years in, we added to the complexity by adopting three more little ones with hard stories.

Let's just say our marriage was complicated. I couldn't even remember the last time I'd walked leisurely down a sidewalk holding my man's hand.

And that's when my admiration of this lovely couple's reality became stinging disappointment with my own. *What about me?*

237

I wanted to scream. *What about my needs? It's not fair!* I almost stomped my feet and pouted. This wasn't what I'd signed up for.

Unfortunately, this wasn't the last time I wrestled disappointment with my reality. I dreamed of a marriage and family that looked like a Hallmark movie, but I ended up with something pulled from a daytime soap opera.

When discontent threatens to poison peace, I know I have a choice. I can grow bitter and disillusioned. Or I can look to Jesus, choosing to see Him as the only perfect Lover of my heart. When I trust Him to meet my needs, I no longer need to stomp and scream for what I lack.

Jesus told His followers, "Whoever wants to be my disciple must deny themselves and take up their cross daily and follow me. For whoever wants to save their life will lose it, but whoever loses their life for me will save it" (Luke 9:23–24).

It's not easy, learning to deny myself and love like Jesus does. Truth is, I'd rather whine, complain, and demand my own way. And yet Jesus chose to lose His life, not to save it. He chose to love us, not to resent us.

To live is to die. To love is to serve. And to find what your heart needs most is to take up the day's cross, grab Jesus's hand, and follow Him wherever He goes. When your marriage looks like a movie—and especially when it doesn't.

PRAYER

Lord, my life doesn't look like what I had imagined it would. It is more difficult and complicated, but this is how You're showing me more of Yourself. Help me to live and love as You do. May I take up the day's cross and grab Your hand, ready to follow You wherever You lead. Amen.

Day 90

the purpose of church

Share each other's burdens, and in this way obey the law of Christ.

Galatians 6:2 NLT

We walked down the back alley to the church, balancing a topped-off bowl of cucumber salad and our bag of paper goods, our Bibles wedged between paper plates and an unruly stack of napkins. Heat blistered up from the street and radiated down from a cloudless sky.

This alley owns a portion of my heart now. It's a strange extension of our home, its lines and dips now grafted into my long-term memory. It's part of what I'll grab years from now when I want to remember this particular life season—with young kids who aren't too young, our long days and short years, and the brick building at the end of the alley where we wrestled against His goodness arriving in the most inconvenient ways.

Six years ago I wondered if church really mattered—"showing up doesn't make someone a Christian" and all that. I asked Abba the hard questions, awaiting vindication, very sure He'd let me clean off the hook. He looked me square in the eyes and with so much kindness began to answer. He still hasn't stopped to take a breath.

God is showing me the family He has provided for me on Sunday mornings, Monday evenings, and the lucky Friday nights.

He's showing me the profound honor of growing roots into the same rocky soil as people I might not always feel particularly inclined toward. He's steering me toward brothers and sisters who refuse to turn away from my shadowy heart. He's sending me people willing to endure my incessant rabbit trails along with my endless questions and hypotheticals.

God is refining me through the ministry of easy laughter, frustrating meetings, and haphazard potlucks.

We get it so wrong, but He keeps showing up for us, often disguised as one another. He reveals Himself, quite improbably, through humans who struggle to get along, who have different opinions, who need a break and want an out. He delivers first aid through His wild, unruly love wrapped in the human flesh of maxed-out misfits.

I know this because on our walk back up the alley after Bible study, my seven-year-old wrecked his bike, and I got to be the one who washed and bandaged his cuts. I, the one who had spent a solid hour earlier that same day grieving my unrecognized entitlement. I, the one who sometimes speaks sarcastically to my children. I, the one who so easily slips beneath the weight of martyrdom. *I* got to tend his wounds. I got to bear a tiny bit of his pain, never mind my shaky qualifications for being worthy of the job.

This "mommy" moment is but a tiny pixel in the frame of why a community of saints matters.

This is church.

It's you and me, bearing burdens, celebrating victories, and trading recipes when a certain lemon-berry dessert demands to be shared.

You might be a padded-chair sort of person, and I might lean a bit "Jonathan Edwards" in my proclivity for a solid walnut pew. Maybe you meet in a school or your church happens every Tuesday at ten. It doesn't matter one lick.

What God wants for us when it comes to community is that when we wreck our bike, there's someone not far behind who will drop what they're holding and sprint to us. What He intends is an earthly family made up of ordinary kids who, empowered only by their Dad's love, will scoop us up when we're hurting, walk our bike down the back alley when we can't ride, kiss our sweaty cheeks, and carry us home.

PRAYER

Lord, I am ever grateful for community, for Your church. We often get it so wrong, but when we get it even close to right, it is life-giving, healing, transformative. Thank You for the gift of what church can be. In Your name, Father God, amen.

Day 91

family . . . whatever that looks like

> Just as our bodies have many parts and each part has a special function, so it is with Christ's body. We are many parts of one body, and we all belong to each other.
>
> Romans 12:4–5 NLT

We all have an idea in our head of what a family "should" look like, to some degree. And usually our own doesn't fit the bill.

Mom, dad, 2.5 kids. Dog, house, car(s), job(s). Family meals. Happiness.

It's the rare family that looks like this picture, isn't it? Yet somehow, it's what many of us conjure up immediately upon hearing the word *family*.

Both my parents and my husband's parents are divorced, which means our kids have four separate sets of grandparents. It can get tricky at times—especially with things like juggling four separate holiday gatherings, grandparents' day at school, and sometimes awkward same-room situations. It doesn't look quite like I always thought it would, and it doesn't look like my own childhood. However, figuring out how to explain it to our kids is just part of what it looks like to be in our family.

In the same way that all bodies are different, no two exactly alike, all families are different. Diverse. Unique. And no two are the same. My kids are growing up with four sets of grandparents, and all of us together are still a family—as is your own family. Whether you're

- A single mom of one child
- Two parents with six children
- A daughter caring for an aging parent
- A parent of adopted children
- A childless married couple
- A grandparent raising your children's children

Or any number of other configurations. No matter what your family looks like, it's a family. Maybe for you, family is a cousin or your mom or a favorite aunt. Maybe you've been estranged from your family for good reasons. You're not out a family just because yours may not be close or look like the picture in your head, because God's family holds us all.

The thing about being one of God's children is that when you're in, you're in for life . . . and then forever. You're never family-less. You are a part of the body, and we all belong to one another.

PRAYER

God, for my loud, messy, weird, wonderful family, I give You thanks. It might not look perfect, but it's mine and it's enough. Thank You for the gift of my greater family— Yours. God, You are Maker, Redeemer, Healer, and Provider for all families. Bless the ones who cannot be together, those who would like to be under one roof but are unable to do so. Bring all of us peace. Amen.

Day 92

it's okay to not be okay

He makes me lie down in green pastures,
he leads me beside quiet waters,
    he refreshes my soul.
He guides me along the right paths
    for his name's sake.
Even though I walk
    through the darkest valley,
I will fear no evil,
    for you are with me;
your rod and your staff,
    they comfort me.

Psalm 23:2–4

I sat beside her on the couch, and she didn't even look up. I was visiting a friend who was not okay.

It was more than a bad day; it was a sad season for her.

But I wasn't deterred from my mission to cheer her up. And I tried *everything*. I suggested going for a walk, reminded her of good times, quoted inspiring Scripture, and offered to play worship music.

I got an occasional head nod and a shrug.

As I sat there in silence, I thought back to the days when I haven't been okay. Some days I could name the pain I felt, and other days I couldn't. And I remembered what I needed the most.

So I did what I should have done in the first place: I hugged her and whispered in her ear, "It's okay to not be okay."

She sighed in relief. Permission to not be okay is sometimes exactly what we need.

We sat in comfortable silence for a long time. I reminded her that God loved these days the best—the ones we can't fix on our own. Because He is there with us. He doesn't always change our circumstances, and we don't always feel something new, but we aren't alone. Sometimes that's all we need.

She wiped away a single tear and whispered, "Thank you." By the time I left, I hadn't done much, but it was enough.

Today you might not be okay. You might be facing a mountain of sadness or impossibility. You might be walking through a valley of despair. You might not even know why you aren't okay. You might be looking at a scary diagnosis, experiencing a financial disaster, or struggling with a wayward child.

I've experienced all of the above.

These are the moments we wrestle and do everything we can think of to resolve the struggle in our soul. And life sort of feels like quicksand—the harder we struggle, the deeper we sink. The days seem dark and lonely, and our soul is crushed by the heaviness of despair.

But only one thing can refresh and renew and save our soul, and that's the Word. Yet God's Word is often the last place we turn. It's crazy to think a book with words can be the answer, but the Word of God is alive, and it cuts to the broken places and heals what we cannot.

The situation or struggle might not dissolve overnight, but we can find solace and comfort in the words He's left for us.

There's only one place to restore our soul and find comfort, and that's in the quiet place at Jesus's feet, where it's okay to not be okay.

Because one day He will make everything okay.

PRAYER

Jesus, I am not okay. Thank You for the permission to feel that despair, and thank You for the antidote to it— You and Your Word. You are with me, and I don't have to lean into the fear; rather, I can lean into Your guidance, even through the darkest valleys. Point me to the right places in Scripture that will speak to my pain and soothe my weary soul. May the truth that one day You will make everything okay sink deeply into my soul. In Your name I pray, amen.

The thing about being one
of God's children is that
when you're in,

you're in for life . . .

and then forever.
You're never family-less.
You are a part of the body,
and we all belong to one another.

—ANNA E. RENDELL

Day 93

the reason you're in the wilderness

I am the LORD your God,
who teaches you what is good for you
and leads you along the paths you should follow.

Isaiah 48:17 NLT

I've experienced many times in the wilderness with God, but it was after college graduation when I first learned my time in the wilderness was for a purpose and only for a season.

I graduated from Baylor with high aspirations. I studied abroad my last semester of college, so I wasn't submitting resumes. I was determined to move to Europe and work my way up the corporate ladder, but my life didn't go as planned.

I won't bore you with the details, but I humbly moved back home after graduation, tirelessly looked for a job for six months, and came to the end of myself.

God used this very hard time to purify me, to change my heart and my plans, to shift my focus toward Him and get me plugged into a church, and to put me in a spiritual leadership role for the first time. He also provided a job in the place, the time, and the way He would get the most glory.

If it wasn't for this wilderness time, I never would have lived in Arkansas, met my husband, changed my career path, worked for a ministry, led a Bible study, or spent time in God's Word searching for His truth. I learned that going through the wilderness with Jesus is a gift and always has a purpose.

Your time in the wilderness is not a punishment or a mistake, but is a holy and needed time for you to be empowered for God's calling.

God's first invitation for His children to go through the wilderness comes in Exodus 3, and the purpose is so they will worship Him. God called Moses and shared His plan to rescue the Israelites. God gave the map to the promised land—through the wilderness.

I can see us in the Israelites. They were God's chosen people, and we are too. He calls them His children, just as He does with us, and He loved them through the wilderness, even with all their complaining and neediness.

God called His people into the wilderness to worship, not to wander, and the time they spent there was proof that God was rescuing them.

The wilderness is also an important part of your path to the promised land. It actually enables you to dwell in your promised land. No one feels comfortable in the wilderness. Comfort isn't God's reason for leading you there; sanctification is.

The purpose in those seasons is to reveal your need for Him, to purify you, and to make room for His holiness in you. Even if it feels as if you have been left out in the middle of nowhere, you are being guided to a specific destination with a specific intention—to become like Him in holiness.

Wilderness seasons are opportunities to see God feed you, light your path, fight for you, provide for you, and become the all-encompassing fire you need. God calls His children, even His very own Son, into the wilderness for a brief time to prove we are His, to allow us to believe in His miracles, to show us how much He can do and how He will take care of us.

So don't fight the invitation to go through the wilderness with the Lord. It doesn't scare Him. Know that you're still walking the path toward your promised land and that this is an adventure between you and God. He is with you through it all.

Thank You, Lord, for being big enough to handle my wilderness, and for doing good within it. Uncomfortable and scary as it is, may I have the grace and fortitude to follow You into the wilderness. I won't fight You. Let's go on an adventure—together. Amen.

Day 94

loving the unkind

For when I am weak, then I am strong.

2 Corinthians 12:10

I finished my faith essay on an airplane, writing on scrap paper to capture my thoughts. "Your editor needs it now," I was told, so I hurried to finish. Then there it was—an eight-hundred-word piece published for the world to see.

My best writing ever? Not by a long shot. Perfection is a high bar, in writing for sure, but also in life. Yet when I looked over readers' comments about the essay, I was struck by one distinct element—their unkindness.

I'd written about my daughter's experience as a Muslim convert who daily wears the hijab. She gets stares and glares, especially in airports and on planes. *Rather than suspect her,* I wrote, *let's do the courageous thing and love—across faiths, across race, across cultures. To love, yes, like Jesus.* It wasn't an original thesis, but I sought to be positive. Then I read the comments.

Talk about hate. This was hate unleashed. A spewing fire hose of put-downs, vitriol, ridicule, ire—I can't list enough negative words—gushed forth without apology.

This woman is an arrogant fool.

They are both idiots.

The woman is dumber than the daughter.

251

You should have raised her better.

I wasn't hurt by such comments. I just wondered what kind of person feels justified unloading on another human being with no regard whatsoever for that person's basic humanity. Internet anger? That's the term for the unkindness flung daily across the blogosphere. The weapons? Hateful words.

We all experience it. On the internet, for sure. Verbal abuse also happens, however, in homes and families. You might be reading this, and this very day you might've been put down by a family member, coworker, or friend—someone who, by all rights, should be offering not hate but love.

So how should we react? The apostle Paul urged us to rely on God's strength, not on our own. Paul says, "That is why, for Christ's sake, I delight in weaknesses, in insults, in hardships, in persecutions, in difficulties. For when I am weak, then I am strong" (2 Cor. 12:10).

God indeed knows when you've been stung by someone's unkindness. So don't lash back. Instead, give your hurt to the Lord. And to the other person? Respond in love, even if you feel weak—knowing that in your weakness, you're strong in God.

In His love we build bridges, not walls. That is what the world needs.

PRAYER

Lord, people can be so unkind, and it hurts to be on the receiving end of it. You say that it's in weakness that Your strength can shine, so God, bring me strength enough to react in love. Help me take deep breaths, and let Your peace—the kind that surpasses understanding—fill my soul before I respond. Let me be shaped by Your kindness and help me to react in the strength of Your love. Amen.

Day 95

a secret to parenting tweens, teens, and beyond

A gentle answer deflects anger,
but harsh words make tempers flare.

Proverbs 15:1 NLT

Motherhood reveals our desperate need for God. We beg for wisdom, offering unceasing prayers rooted in faith, hope, and love. We hold children tightly as we pray for their future, letting go slowly as they slowly grow up.

So how is it that days last forever while years go by in a blink? It seems like overnight your daughter is asking for makeup and going bra shopping, and your son's voice is changing. You begin to wonder if hormones snatched your once-agreeable child, and challenges you never imagined emerge: erratic mood swings, disobedience, poor choices.

During one of those difficult challenges, I was at a loss on how to confront my son over something I suspected but could not prove. My husband was away on an extended work assignment, and I was solo parenting.

I longed to avoid what I had seen happen in confronting older children: they lie, shut down, or push you away. Was there *any* approach that would lead to truth? How was I to get to the heart of my child?

For weeks, I prayed. I sought the counsel of youth leaders and friends to no avail. My prayers became increasingly urgent, begging God for wisdom not yet revealed.

But then, like Elijah in 1 Kings 19:11–13, I heard God in a whisper: *Be gentle.* After thrashing for weeks, I knew I needed to approach this hard conversation differently, with no anger, accusations, or ready lecture.

Beginning by acknowledging my helplessness, I explained my desire not to put him in a position to lie or drive a wedge between us. Our conversation was tender and gut-wrenchingly honest, and before I could finish, he spilled everything, his countenance expressing welcomed relief.

It was gentleness that opened the door to his heart.

As parents, it's understandable sometimes to react to our children's behavior with anger, harshness, or disappointment. But just as it is God's kindness that leads us to repentance, it is our gentleness that can bridge the gap between parent and child and remind us that we are all beloved children of God.

PRAYER

Lord, at times it is so hard not to react harshly! I know it's worth it, I know the benefits are tenfold, but in this moment and this situation, I want to be anything but gentle. God, help me breathe. Help me to be kind, to show Your love by being gentle, and to lead my child(ren) back to You. Amen.

Day 96

wrestling well through a hard season

And he who searches our hearts knows the mind of the Spirit, because the Spirit intercedes for God's people in accordance with the will of God.

Romans 8:27

"Have you said goodbye?" My friend's words were gentle yet pulsed with concern.

My eyes closed to hold the tears at bay; I bit my lip to quell its quiver. My sister's death was eighteen months behind me, but I was still slogging through the muck of grief. I didn't want to hear this question, much less ponder and act on it. Saying goodbye meant letting go, and I was not ready to face the finality that would bring.

Three days later, my friend and I went on a getaway with a few other friends. Her question had not left me since she had released it into the air, so I opened my journal in the quiet hours of the last morning of our trip and started writing. My pencil scratched furiously, unspoken words pouring from its tip. Tears dripped down my nose as the things left unsaid made their way from the shadows of my heart to the page.

When I finished, I turned to look at my friend, and in that moment I realized what I had done.

"I just said goodbye."

The words had barely escaped my lips when a guttural sob rose from the depths of me. Leaning into my friend's embrace, I mourned the finality of what had just occurred: I had let my sister go.

In the weeks following that day, I experienced a more freeing peace than I had felt since my sister passed away. The tension of feeling responsible for preserving her memory dissipated. I realized that the essence of who she was will always be accessible to me and to those who knew her. Though she is no longer with us physically, the memories we shared with her are ours forever.

Grief isn't linear; once you've experienced loss, it becomes a part of you. Some days it is more visible than others. Some days the pain incapacitates you; other days it recedes enough that you almost forget it's there.

Perhaps you're in the midst of circumstances where you're having to wrestle with God through the night as Jacob did. Here's what I know:

Grieve what should have been, and tell God how you really feel.

As Christians, we may believe that our messy, negative emotions—sadness, anger, fear, and anxiety—are not appropriate, and we may try to ignore or suppress them. But God can handle your full range of emotions. Voice your emotions through prayer or journaling; the Holy Spirit waits to comfort you in your heartache.

There is hope, friend. I know it may not seem like it now, but it is there. If you squint, you may catch a glimpse of it in the distance. Hold on, the dawn is coming.

PRAYER

Lord, I don't even have the words to tell You all that I'm feeling. There is grief and pain and anger, and I know You can handle the full range of my emotions. Hold me, Lord. Hold me and sustain me until I can get to hope. Amen.

Day 97

counting gratefuls

Never stop praying. Be thankful in all circumstances, for this is God's will for you who belong to Christ Jesus.

1 Thessalonians 5:17–18 NLT

Nighttime was the hardest after my husband left. During the day, work, church, and mom stuff distracted me from my harsh reality, but when the sun went down, so did my hope. Despair seeped in like smoke and choked my peace. The empty space next to me in bed felt like a grave, and in some ways I guess it was. My marriage was dead, and many nights I wished I was too. I felt like Job on his ash heap. "When I lie down I think, 'How long before I get up?' The night drags on, and I toss and turn until dawn" (Job 7:4).

After weeks of waking up exhausted from carrying the weight of the world in my dreams, I sensed God's gentle nudging. *What's right about your life, Lee? Count your gratefuls and find my peace.*

That night I started muttering my thanks to God for anything that came to mind. I thanked Him for my sweet pup snuggled up against my hip. I thanked Him for Sonic Diet Cokes with lemon. I thanked Him for toilet paper and air-conditioning. For a sale on shampoo just when my stash ran low. For that call from a friend at just the right moment. For light traffic on the way to work. I

257

thanked Him for my sons and how I'm still their momma, even if I'm not their daddy's wife.

Once I got started, the stream of thanksgiving flowed, smooth and easy, into peaceful sleep.

"In peace I will lie down and sleep, for you alone, Lord, make me dwell in safety" (Ps. 4:8).

When my alarm chirped, I climbed out of bed with a better mindset. Less dread. Less worry. Less despair. More gratitude.

The words in Psalm 30:5 about joy coming in the morning began to feel true to me. Though I continued to struggle with feelings of dread and despair, I no longer wallowed in them. I began to understand my hope was secure because it was built on Christ, the One who never leaves me or forsakes me.

Closing my day with thanksgiving didn't fix my problems, but it helped me fix my eyes on Jesus.

And the more I fixed my eyes on Jesus, "the author and perfecter of faith" (Heb. 12:2 NASB), the more He could bring me to a wholeness I had never known. A wholeness that defied my broken circumstances.

> Therefore we do not lose heart. Though outwardly we are wasting away, yet inwardly we are being renewed day by day. For our light and momentary troubles are achieving for us an eternal glory that far outweighs it all. So we fix our eyes not on what is seen, but on what is unseen, since what is seen is temporary, but what is unseen is eternal. (2 Cor. 4:16–18)

Are nights hard for you, friend? Do you wake up worn out from your worries and heartache? Maybe you're going through an unwanted divorce like I did. Maybe your child is running from God. Maybe someone you love is battling cancer. Maybe the loneliness is suffocating.

Whatever is stealing your peace, counting your gratefuls will help you take it back.

PRAYER

God, I have been abandoned, and my peace has been stolen from me. I am so weary as I try to figure out how to do life again. Come be with me in the night, when everything becomes magnified, and in my loneliness, carry me. Help call to mind even the smallest of things for which I can give thanks, and restore peace in my soul and mind again. Amen.

Day 98

everyday friendship

Therefore, as God's chosen ones, holy and dearly loved, put
on compassion, kindness, humility, gentleness, and patience,
bearing with one another and forgiving one another if anyone
has a grievance against another. Just as the Lord has forgiven
you, so you are also to forgive. Above all, put on love, which
is the perfect bond of unity.

Colossians 3:12–14 CSB

One of my closest friends moved halfway across the country,
and as we were chatting on the phone one day, we came to the
conclusion that friendships will always be a thing. No matter
how old we are or what stage of life we are in, they will always
be a thing that requires effort, thought, care, and intentionality.

Often we overcomplicate what godly, authentic friendships
are supposed to look like. We think they are supposed to be
perfect, with no tension. We glamorize them and imagine them
to be something that God never intended them to be.

I'm almost forty now, and my friendships are a bit different in this season of life than they were in my twenties. Back
then, college was this bubble where we did life together. Be-
sides going to class, we studied the Word in small groups, went
on mission trips, worshiped and prayed, and played a ton of
games. It was such a sweet time when my faith grew by leaps
and bounds.

Life at my age is different. It's often filled with ministry, career, marriage, kids, and busy schedules. It can be a bit overwhelming if I let it, and it can be what keeps me disconnected and isolated.

The enemy wants us to be alone and lonely and discouraged. But the Lord created us out of community—Father, Son, and Holy Spirit—and He created us in His image. From the very beginning, God's heart was for us to be in community with Himself and with others.

Friendship is as simple as loving each other simply. Sometimes it's weddings and funerals and fun events and traveling. But for the most part, my friends and I are not living out fancy lives together. We take walks or go grocery shopping. We hang out at their kids' sports and arts events. There's usually food and coffee involved. There's even some cleaning and laundry getting done. We get creative in every season. We extend grace and patience and forgiveness to each other.

It's the everyday friendships that I hold dear to my heart. They give strength and foster unity, and I see Christ in them. Friendships will always be a thing, but I know they are worth the effort and intentionality it takes to have a community around me.

PRAYER

God, thank You for creating community, for creating us to be in community with You and with other people. I'm grateful for the everyday friendships I have now, but I remember the days when even that was lacking and how You provided. Help me to treasure what You've given me and to put forth the required effort, thought, care, and intentionality it takes to be a good friend. Amen.

Day 99

hope in the dark in-between

I will never forget this awful time,
    as I grieve over my loss.
Yet I still dare to hope
    when I remember this:
The faithful love of the LORD never ends!
    His mercies never cease.
Great is his faithfulness;
    his mercies begin afresh each morning.
I say to myself, "The LORD is my inheritance;
    therefore, I will hope in him!"

Lamentations 3:20–24 NLT

My hair is growing back. Little wisps have suddenly appeared around my face, darker brown than the rest of my hair, like someone accidentally scuffed a marker across my temple. I didn't see them a week ago, but now they are there, and I wonder what else is being restored.

The hair began falling out in clumps last winter, long strands whirling around the shower floor and clogging up my detangler brush. When I finally went to the dermatologist, she asked if there had been any stressors in my life a month before this began.

A month earlier, I had gotten into my husband's car on a cold Christmas Eve to go look at lights. It was the last thing I did without pain for months. The doctors said nerve pain is like nothing else, and they were right. Screaming pain seared from my lower back to my toes, and I once wondered if cutting them off could possibly hurt more. Months of physical therapy kept me from the surgeon's knife, but those months were hard to retrieve.

So, any stressors? Yeah, maybe.

The hair was just the flashing alert signal of what was happening inside. Work, family, writing, hobbies, everything—all of it was uprooted and rearranged to accommodate this new me. Unable to perform normal daily functions, I felt useless and incapable—like I wasn't pulling my appointed load in the universe and everyone else had to pick up my slack.

The post-injury me lost herself in a dark world of lies about my usefulness and fears about my future.

My life would be divided in two by this event. Before injury and after injury, like my personal BC and AD. Isn't this true more often than we realize? Something comes along, and we may not even realize at the time that it's going to be a big thing—like getting into a car for a Christmas light expedition.

It becomes a big thing, a massive thing. It invades our life, changing everything we thought we knew. I've had dividing points before this. A parent's death. A life-altering surgery. A child's wandering away. We sit in that space between life before and life after, not knowing what it will look like on the other side of the door, not truly believing we'll even get there because the pain of the empty space is so great and the darkness is so deep.

Then one day we see wisps of hope curling around our faces. They weren't there before. We didn't think we'd ever see them again. But there they are. They greet us, gently telling us that we've crossed over the threshold into what life will be from now on. It will be different, but that does not mean it will be bad. We take the things we've learned in that in-between space, and we venture into the new, newly equipped.

I will never forget sitting in that place of in-between. I will never get back what was before, but I will forever feel the presence of the One who met me and embraced me in the in-between.

And I know I will be there again sometime, yet I still dare to hope. I dare to believe in restoration. New hair is new hope, and isn't it like God to offer those beautiful wisps of joyful hope when you forgot to expect it?

And hey, it's not even gray.

PRAYER

God, I need new hope. As long as You're guiding and leading my heart, I will dare to believe in restoration, in joy, in a space beyond this in-between place. I'll be looking for signs of growth where there once were none, and for peace in the process. Thank You for being the God of hope. Amen.

hope grows under the surface

So we fix our eyes not on what is seen, but on what is unseen, since what is seen is temporary, but what is unseen is eternal.

2 Corinthians 4:18

I'm no gardener, but this past October I planted tulip bulbs in the ground and shared more from the batch with some dear friends. As winter approached, I bought amaryllis bulbs, planted two in pots, and gave away even more. I wasn't looking for a new hobby, and I don't revel working in the dirt.

I planted because I needed to believe that something as ugly and dry as a bulb could surprise me by sprouting, growing, and blooming. I needed the possibility of the picture of resurrection, and I needed witnesses to walk along with me in it.

Hope is fragile, and it can be elusive. As my kids grow into their late teens, and as I seek vocation and new meaning from life, I find so much unknown, and it scares me. We are each of us walking winding roads these days, with a mixture of joys and lessons-still-to-learn. It's hard to see where these roads might lead, and trust has never been my strongest suit. It was so much easier when the kids were younger and I could choose everything for them—when the world was as small as their elementary school and soccer fields. It's different now, and so are they, and so am I.

Now, when the world feels utterly unpredictable, I need to hold hope in my hands.

265

My friends and I agreed to plant the bulbs, dry and dead-looking as they were, and to encourage one another through the winter and spring. There's so much that happens just under the surface that you can't see, after all. And just because you can't see what's happening *doesn't mean it's not happening.*

So we'll wait and we'll watch. We'll see the amaryllis bulbs poke through first, in the warmth of our homes. They'll bloom red and joyful in our kitchens as the sunlight streams through the windows.

But it's the tulip bulbs outside that will mostly occupy my thoughts through a cold and snowy New England winter. The little bulbs are already working hard, out of my sight and without my help, using what's been inside them all along to burst forth into something amazing. By the time I see the evidence of their green shoots, so much of the work will already have been done without me.

I planted them, but God will make them grow.

It takes a great force of faith to envision spring in the midst of winter, to imagine a shoot coming through the cold, dark earth, to know it's been in process all along. This is the way God is calling me to operate in my life today, to believe even when it's hard, even if I can't always see.

He is making something beautiful just outside my reach. In this winter of my life, He is turning my thoughts to spring.

PRAYER

Lord, what I planted, make grow. Give me hope to see even the smallest seeds growing, getting ready to bloom brightly. Give me faith to envision spring in the midst of winter, to know that You are at work in the dark, in the cold, in the hard. Help me truly believe that You are making something beautiful just outside of my reach, turning winter to spring. Amen.

index

Note: locators indicate days, not page numbers.

Community
Church, 33, 37, 90
Loneliness, 16, 47, 55
General struggle
Calling, 6, 41, 82
Seasons, 17, 22, 23, 32, 39, 40, 46, 48, 59, 77, 78, 85, 93, 100
Spiritual, 3, 4, 14, 18, 21, 50, 62, 66, 69
Grief
Death, 58, 64, 81, 84, 96
Sadness/lament, 16, 30, 43, 49, 92
Suicide, 86
Widow, 10, 72
Identity
Cultural, 65, 68
Self, 2, 13, 56, 70, 94
Shame, 15, 87
Injustice, 11, 24, 28, 36, 44, 52, 65, 68

Mental health
Anxiety, 1, 12, 19
Depression, 1, 71
Midlife, 34, 45, 73, 76
Motherhood
Blended family, 31, 91
Infertility, 20, 74, 88
Miscarriage, 7
Older children, 60, 80, 95
Pregnancy loss, 64
Special needs, 53, 75
Struggle, 26, 29, 38, 42, 55
Physical pain, 27, 51, 99
Relationship
Friendship, 8, 9, 25, 35, 57, 63, 98
Marriage, 5, 72, 89, 97
Singleness, 67
Self-care, 54, 61, 79, 83

about the contributors

Karina Allen is devoted to helping women live out their unique calling and building authentic community through practical application of Scripture in an approachable, winsome manner. Connect with her on Instagram at @karina268.

Lisa-Jo Baker is the bestselling author of *Never Unfriended, Surprised by Motherhood*, and *The Middle Matters: Why That (Extra)Ordinary Life Looks Really Good on You*. She is also a cohost of the *Out of the Ordinary* podcast. Find her at lisajo baker.com and @lisajobaker on Instagram.

Lucretia Berry is the creator of Brownicity.com. She is a wife, mom of three, and a former college professor, whose passion for racial healing led her to author *What LIES Between Us: Fostering First Steps Toward Racial Healing* and to speak at TEDx Charlotte and Q Ideas Charlotte. Find her at brownicity .com and @lucretiaberry on Instagram.

Kaitlyn Bouchillon is a writer who is learning to see God's goodness in the beautiful ordinary of right now. She is the author of *Even If Not: Living, Loving, and Learning in the*

In-Between, and she'll never turn down an iced latte. Find her at kaitlynbouchillon.com and @kaitlyn_bouch on Instagram.

Stephanie Bryant is the cofounder of (in)courage and a podcaster at the #JesusLedAdventurePodcast. She enjoys spending her days with her husband and their miracle daughter on their farm. Find Stephanie on Instagram at @stephaniesbryant and at stephaniebryant.me.

Dawn Camp is an Atlanta-based photographer, wife, essential oil enthusiast, homeschooling mom to eight, and Mimi to four. She is the author of *It All Began in a Garden* and has edited four book compilations, including *With Love, Mom.* Connect with her at dawncamp.com and on Instagram at @dawncamp.

Kerry Campbell is a Catholic-Christian preschool music teacher, church singer, full-time noticer, and mom to two almost-grown kids. She's letting the details of her life inform her wider view near Boston, and she writes about it all at mylittleepiphan ies.com and @kerrycampbellwrites on Instagram.

Mary Carver is a writer and speaker who lives for good books, spicy queso, and television marathons—but lives because of God's grace. She writes about giving up on perfect and finding truth in unexpected places at marycarver.com and @marycarver on Instagram. Mary and her husband live in Kansas City with their two daughters.

Grace P. Cho is the (in)courage editorial manager. In the middle of her years in church ministry, she sensed God moving her toward writing, to use her words to lead. She coaches writers, mentors leaders, and believes that telling our stories can change the world. Connect with her at @gracepcho on Instagram.

Michele Cushatt is a three-time tongue cancer survivor, mama of children from "hard places," and (reluctant) expert on pain, trauma, and the deep human need for connection. She's the author of *Relentless: The Unshakeable Presence of a God Who Never Leaves*. Michele lives in Colorado with her husband and their six children. Find her at michelecushatt.com and @michele cushatt on Instagram.

Robin Dance is the author of *For All Who Wander*, is married to her college sweetheart, and is as Southern as sugar-shocked tea. An empty nester with a full life, she's determined to age with grace and laugh at the days to come. Connect with her at robindance.me and @robindance.me on Instagram.

Holley Gerth is a bestselling author who loves encouraging the hearts of women through words. She does so through her books like *You're Already Amazing* and *Fiercehearted*. Holley is a beloved daughter of God, wife to Mark, mama to Lovelle, and nana to Ellie. Find her at holleygerth.com and @holleygerth on Instagram.

Dorina Lazo Gilmore is a blogger, speaker, and author of *Glory Chasers* and *Flourishing Together*. She specializes in helping people navigate grief and flourish in community. An award-winning children's author, Dorina has also served as a journalist, missionary, and social entrepreneur. She and her husband are raising three brave girls. Find her at dorinagilmore.com and @dorinagilmore on Instagram.

Bonnie Gray is a wife, mom to two boys, and the author of *Whispers of Rest* and *Finding Spiritual Whitespace*. An inspirational speaker who has been featured at Relevant Magazine and Christianity Today, she's guided thousands to detox stress and experience God's love through soul care. Find her at thebonnie gray.com and @thebonniegray on Instagram.

Amber C. Haines is the author of *Wild in the Hollow*, and has four sons, a guitar-playing husband, and rare friends. She loves the funky, the narrative, and the dirty South. She finds community among the broken and wants to know your story. Find her at amberchaines.com and @amberchaines on Instagram.

Liz Curtis Higgs is a former Bad Girl, grateful for the grace God offers. She's the happy wife of Bill and the proud mom of two grown-up kids. She is the author of nearly forty books. Find her at lizcurtishiggs.com and facebook.com/lizcurtishiggs.

Alia Joy writes about her life with bipolar disorder, as well as about grief, faith, marriage, poverty, race, and keeping fluent in the language of hope in her book *Glorious Weakness: Discovering God in All We Lack*. She lives in Central Oregon with her husband, her tiny Asian mother, and her three kids. Visit her at www.aliajoy.com and @aliajoyh on Instagram.

Tasha Jun is a dreamer, a Hapa girl, wife to Matt, and mama to three little tender warriors. A coffee-drinker, storyteller, and kimchi-eater, she was made to walk where cultures collide, on dirt roads and carefully placed cobblestone streets. Jesus is her heartbeat. Find her at @tashajunb on Instagram and tashajun.com.

Becky Keife loves serving as the community manager for (in)courage. She is the author of *No Better Mom for the Job* and is also a speaker, editor, and blessed mama of three spirited boys. Connect with her on Instagram at @beckykeife.

Aliza Latta is a Canadian writer, journalist, and artist, who is a huge fan of telling stories. She writes about faith and young adulthood at alizalatta.com, and is the author of the novel *Come Find Me, Sage Parker*. Find her on Instagram at @alizalatta.

Jennifer Dukes Lee and her husband live on the family farm, raising crops, pigs, and two humans. She is the author of *Love*

Idol and *It's All Under Control,* and is a fan of dark chocolate, emojis, eighties music, bright lipstick, and Netflix binges.

Ticcoa Leister is a Carolina girl transplanted to Texas. An introvert who survived her Worst Best Year on a 23,461-mile road trip with an extrovert, she writes with the hope that her story will inspire others. Find her at ticcoa.com and @ticcoaleister on Instagram.

Lisa Leonard is a wife and a mom to two boys. In between school and work, they spend their time playing outdoors on the California coast, eating chocolate chip pancakes, tapping tunes on the piano, and choreographing elaborate light saber duels. Lisa also creates handmade jewelry. Find her at lisaleonard.com and @lisaleonard on Instagram.

Elizabeth Manley is a writer, poet, pastor's wife, and mom to seven—four in her arms and three just out of sight. She writes on the intersection of grief and faith and on rediscovering life after loss. Find her at riskingloss.blogspot.com and @elizabeth.manley.writes on Instagram.

Shannan Martin is the author of *Falling Free: Rescued From the Life I Always Wanted* and *The Ministry of Ordinary Places: Waking Up to God's Goodness Around You.* She is the wife of a jail chaplain and mom to four kiddos. She's a big believer in community and salsa and blogs at shannanmartinwrites.com. Find her on Instagram at @shannanwrites.

Lee Merrill is the grateful momma of three adult sons and an enthusiastic cheerleader and teacher to students with special needs. She is the author of *Prayer Gifts While You Wait.* Find her at praywithoutceasing.today and @leebirdpwc on Instagram.

Joanne Moon is a writer and preacher grappling with the intersectionality of spiritual formation and soul care with race, disability, and community. Together with her engineer-pastor husband and three children, they are navigating the adventure that autism brings with God's enduring companionship and the support of family and friends. Find her at jominute.com.

Anjuli Paschall has an MA in Spiritual Formation and Soul Care from Talbot Seminary. She lives in SoCal with her husband and their five children. She is the author of *Stay: Discovering Grace, Freedom, and Wholeness Where You Never Imagined Looking*, writes daily on Instagram at @lovealways.anjuli, and is the founder of @TheMomsWeLoveClub.

Patricia Raybon, an award-winning author and journalist, grew up in a time of hate but found God's love in a time of need. Serving from Colorado, she writes on faith, race, and grace—seeking to inspire healing in Christ. Join her on the journey at patriciaraybon.com.

Anna E. Rendell is the (in)courage digital content manager, and lives in Minnesota with her husband and three kids. She loves a good book and a great latte. Anna is the author of *Pumpkin Spice for Your Soul* and *A Moment of Christmas*. Visit her at annarendell.com and @annaerendell on Instagram.

Michelle Reyes, PhD, is a pastor's wife, German professor, and mom to two. She and her husband planted an urban, multicultural church in Austin, Texas, in 2014. Michelle is passionate about faith, family, and diversity. Read more from her at theartoftaleh.com or @michelleamireyes on Instagram.

Jill Richardson is a speaker, pastor, girl mom, and author. She is a believer in grace, restoration, Earl Grey, and dark chocolate. Connect with her at jillmrichardson.com and @jillmrichardson2 on Instagram.

Deidra Riggs is a national speaker and the author of *Every Little Thing: Making a World of Difference Right Where You Are* and *One: Unity in a Divided World.* Follow Deidra on Instagram at @deidrariggs and at deidrariggs.com.

Bev Rihtarchik is the founder and president of Redeemer Christian Foundation, Inc., which supports Christian education for orphans and impoverished children in the Middle East. She writes weekly at walkingwellwithgod.blogspot.com. Her desire is that her "life arrow" always points toward God.

Jen Schmidt encourages women to embrace both the beauty and bedlam of their everyday lives at beautyandbedlam.com and @jenschmidt_beautyandbedlam on Instagram. A speaker, worship leader, and author of *Just Open the Door: How One Invitation Can Change a Generation,* Jen lives in North Carolina with her husband and five children.

Catherine Segars is a wife of one, mother of five, actor, writer, singer, speaker, and Jesus-lovin' homeschool teacher. An award-winning performer and playwright, Catherine hung up her costumes to pursue motherhood full-time. She has returned to her creative roots with a dynamic blogcast called *That Drama Girl.* Find her at catherinesegars.com and @catherinesegars on Instagram.

Faith Griffin Sims is a mom of six and "Mia" to seventeen grandchildren. She writes about grief, suicide loss, and living life with hope. She lives near Atlanta with her husband of forty-two years and their two youngest children. Connect with her at faithonthejourney.com and @faithgriffinsims on Instagram.

Kristen Strong, author of *Girl Meets Change,* writes as a friend offering meaningful encouragement for each season of life so you can see it with hope instead of worry. She and her

US Air Force veteran husband, David, have three children and live in Colorado Springs. Find her at chasingblueskies.net and @kristenstrong on Instagram.

Renee Swope is the bestselling author of *A Confident Heart* and a former radio cohost at Proverbs 31 Ministries, where she served in leadership for twenty years. Married to J.J., she lives in North Carolina and enjoys making memories with their three kids. Connect with her at ReneeSwope.com and @reneeswope on Instagram.

Jessica Turner is the author of *Stretched Too Thin: How Working Moms Can Lose the Guilt, Work Smarter and Thrive,* and blogs on TheMomCreative.com. She enjoys connecting with online friends at @jessicanturner on Instagram. Jessica and her husband, Matthew, live in Nashville, Tennessee, with their three children.

Jennifer Ueckert is a mixed media artist living in rural Nebraska. She is married to her patient and supportive husband. Jennifer wants her artwork to reflect the beauty of God. You can read her words and see more of her art at studiojru.com and at @studioJRU on Instagram.

Kristen Welch writes at wearethatfamily.com. She is the author of *Rhinestone Jesus* and *Raising Grateful Kids in an Entitled World* and is the founder of themercyhousekenya.org. Connect with her at @wearethatfamily on Instagram.

S. G. Willoughby is a seventeen-year-old girl who loves to write, read, and have adventures. She is a Lymie, TCK (third culture kid), and discipleship group leader for local girls. Sara lives in Arizona with her family and chocolate labradoodle. Find her on Instagram at @r535blog and at sgwilloughby.com.

Melissa Zaldivar is a social in the world of academics and an academic in the world of socials. Author of *Kingdom Come: Finding Holy in the Here and Now*, she holds a master's in theology, is an Enneagram 6, and lives near Boston. Find her at melissazaldivar.com and @melissazaldivar on Instagram.

f 🐦 📷 📌
@incourage

(in)courage welcomes you

to a place where authentic, brave women
connect deeply with God and others.
Through the power of shared stories and
meaningful resources, (in)courage champions
women and celebrates the strength Jesus gives
to live out our calling as God's daughters.
In the middle of your unfine moments
and ordinary days, you are invited to
become a woman of courage.

Join us at **www.incourage.me**
& connect with us on social media!

DaySpring
LIVE YOUR FAITH

PRAYERS TO SHARE

100 PASS-ALONG NOTES

FOR

Courage

take heart
A PRAYER JOURNAL

Other Take Heart products from (in)courage & DaySpring!

Available from your favorite retailer or **DaySpring.com.**

Be the First to Hear about New Books from Revell!

Sign up for announcements about new and upcoming titles at

RevellBooks.com/SignUp

@RevellBooks

Don't miss out on our great reads!

Revell
a division of Baker Publishing Group
www.RevellBooks.com